"Nothing is more tragic for the witnesses than the burnout of a man or woman of God. What was once a bonfire of vision and passion is reduced, seemingly all of a sudden, to a pile of smoldering embers, and we wonder, *What happened?* In truth, the fire has died down gradually over time, and beware—it can happen to anyone. God wasn't referring only to an ancient blaze on an altar of rocks when He warned, 'Do not let the fire go out.' The altar God desires most is a heart that is fully committed to Him. In *Rekindle the Altar Fire*, Chuck Pierce and Alemu Beeftu teach us from Scripture about the significance of biblical altars and their relevance for us today. If your zeal has cooled in your spiritual life, your family life, your church or your ministry, let this book help you discover why and what you can do about it. Here is an insightful, challenging and inspirational manual for preventing burnout in the first place, or for restoring our heart-altar so the Holy Spirit can reignite His fire within us!"

Dr. Wess Stafford, president emeritus, Compassion International

"In a day when it is easy to be busy for God, Chuck Pierce and Alemu Beeftu understand there is no easier place to lose Jesus than in the temple of religious activity and flurry. Far more than just a great book, *Rekindle the Altar Fire* is 'an anchor within the veil' that calls us back to true covenant and passion for God. *Rekindle the Altar Fire* is a powerful manual that shows us how to keep the fires hot on the altar of our relationship with God."

Dr. Don Crum, Leadership International

"In *Rekindle the Altar Fire*, Chuck Pierce and Alemu Beeftu have done a great service to the Body of Christ. This book leaves one with a passion for the presence of God and the pursuit of holiness that few books have ever achieved. As I read it, God lit a new fire in my own heart."

"Chuck Pierce and Alemu Beeftu are to be commended. *Rekindle the Altar Fire* is a wonderful handbook for those who want to burn with holy fire."

Rekindle
the
Altar
Fire

Rekindle *the* Altar Fire

Making a Place for
GOD'S PRESENCE

CHUCK D. PIERCE
AND ALEMU BEEFTU

Chosen

a division of Baker Publishing Group
Minneapolis, Minnesota

Published by Chosen Books
11400 Hampshire Avenue South
Bloomington, Minnesota 55438
www.chosenbooks.com

Chosen Books is a division of
Baker Publishing Group, Grand Rapids, Michigan

Printed in the United States of America

ISBN 978-0-8007-9979-3 (paperback)
ISBN 978-0-8007-6217-9 (casebound)

Library of Congress Cataloging-in-Publication Control Number: 2020943483

Cover design by Bill Johnson

20 21 22 23 24 25 26   7 6 5 4 3 2 1

To the Kingdom remnant intercessors
and watchmen who build new altars
throughout the world

Contents

You are about to enter a journey of seeing and experiencing revival from a personal, corporate, territorial and generational dimension. Revival is the renewal of one's spirit to regain life and lost power. From ancient times until now, there is one concept of revival that is not usually discussed. The principle of God's altar being central to our lives is the key to the awakening and strengthening of our spirits—the inner, eternal life within us. As you build an altar and sustain the fire deep inside, the outward reflection of that power changes the world around you.

1

Why Build an Altar?

They built the altar of the Lord is a phrase found in every move of God, at every new beginning, at every defining moment in biblical history:

- Noah built an altar
- Abraham built an altar
- Moses built an altar
- Aaron built an altar
- Joshua built an altar
- Samuel built an altar
- Even Saul built an altar unto the Lord God of Israel
- Upon return from the Babylonian captivity, the people built an altar
- And on and on and on

John the Baptist cried in the desert, "I baptize you with water for repentance, but the One coming after me will baptize you with the Holy Spirit and fire." To know this fire and keep it burning within us is the understanding we must have in order to experience a perpetual relationship with God—and a move of God within and around us! The fire of God is a sign of spiritual renewal, consecration and empowerment.

In modern history we have forgotten the importance of God's altar. This book, *Rekindle the Altar Fire,* is a modern-day call and explanation for God's people to find our way back to building His altar, resulting in experiencing His fire, joy and renewal.

Building God's Plan of Worship

Most of us are living in an environment of worldly domination. Perhaps that is why I, Chuck, especially like the story of Gideon. Remember that Gideon was motivated by the oppression of the times: The Israelites were not able to prosper. Whenever they planted crops, the Midianites would invade the land and ruin their harvests for the year ahead. Now think about this: You have worked hard all year and saved enough for the year to come—and you get robbed . . . *year* after *year.*

Finally, you have deep within you a cry that says, *Enough is enough!* God, the Ruler of the universe, and of your harvest, visits you with a solution. The real issue becomes not just knowing what will save you and your family's future, but deciding whether or not to act in faith. Gideon is like most of us—unsure, insecure, fearful and filled with a lack of confidence. When the angel of the Lord appeared to him as he was threshing wheat in a winepress, and commanded him to go and save Israel, Gideon offered excuses and asked for a sign. When the Lord confirmed the sign, the call to save Israel created action within him.

"So Gideon built an altar to the LORD there and called it The LORD Is Peace" (Judges 6:24). In other words, an altar of peace and wholeness had to be established in the midst of the trying and confusing times.

That same night, the Lord gave him instructions to tear down his father's idolatrous altar to Baal and "build a proper kind of altar to the LORD your God on the top of this height" (Judges 6:26).

Here is the scenario. Baal, the most prominent idol mentioned throughout the Bible, was the demonic ruler of Canaan. To destroy Baal's altar, along with the Asherah pole beside it, was certain to incur the wrath of Baal's worshipers as well as anger the demonic presence. This action was a bold declaration that the ruler of that land was being dethroned.

But Gideon obeyed God. At night, with ten of his servants, he tore down the idolatrous altar, built a new altar to God and made a sacrifice upon it.

The next morning, as he expected, the townspeople were furious, and demanded that Gideon be put to death. His father made the logical argument that if Baal were a god, he could defend himself when someone came to break down his altar. The people were silenced, and ultimately Gideon led Israel into battle, gaining freedom from the oppression of the Midianites.

It is time for a generation of Gideons to arise and change the course of nations! *We must have a generation that tears down iniquitous altars. To remove the evil, we must have a generation that builds altars filled with God's uncompromising fire.* It is not enough just to overthrow and defeat the powers in a region. We must then build God's plan of worship. This book will help you understand how to build an altar so that the renewed fire comes to God's people.

Dr. Alemu Beeftu, my co-author for this book, has established the key to seeing a nation shift. He is a man of God from Ethiopia with one desire: to see the fire of God sweeping through nations. We will explain how each individual altar is built to contain this fire. This altar is a place for presenting our sacrifices of worship and praise. The altar of God is not an ancient concept but a necessary element in our worship today. It is a place of anointing, and anointing breaks the yoke of the enemy. The altar is a place of overcoming. The altar is a place of daily communion.

In this book, you will learn much about worship and will be motivated to "go up to a high place," tear down the devil's altar and build God's altar. Now is the time for our generation to build God's altar so that His fire may fall. *Rekindle the Altar Fire* defies any dispensation and says, *Build now! Your future depends on the altar.*

Build, Sacrifice and Commune

God's command to the children of Israel through Moses was to construct altars on which sacrifices and offerings would be placed: "Make an altar of earth for me and sacrifice on it your burnt offerings and fellowship offerings, your sheep and goats and your cattle. Wherever I cause my name to be honored, I will come to you and bless you" (Exodus 20:24).

The reason He commanded altars to be built was to establish a meeting place of relationship. In essence, God was saying, "Honor Me and I will bless you." God was not

14

promising to bless the altars, although wherever His presence is, there is blessing. He was promising to bless the people who built the altars. Every believer in every generation desires that blessing, that fire, to fall from God's throne. Without that fire, we quietly and desperately lead the lives of servants, but not children; hired hands, but not heirs to a Kingdom. That kind of servitude is not what Jesus meant when He said, "I have come that they may have life, and have it to the full" (John 10:10).

Maybe you have thought of the fire that comes from God as passion or drive or enthusiasm. We have chosen the word *fire* intentionally because of its status in the Old and New Testaments as an equivalent for the presence and power of God. From a burning bush that demanded shoes be removed to flaming tongues that amazed the early Church, "our 'God is a consuming fire'" (Hebrews 12:29). That fire, *God's fire*, is what is needed for our personal lives, our families, our churches and our nations if we are to have any hope of burning away the impurities of a people whose lips are close but whose hearts are far from Him.

This is where the use of an altar must be established in our lives on a daily basis. There cannot be a lasting fire without an altar: "For the eyes of the LORD range throughout the earth to strengthen those whose hearts are fully committed to him" (2 Chronicles 16:9). God desires to send *fire*, to strengthen and equip us for every good work; our Holy God wants an altar, a place of pure and wholehearted relationship, where He can meet with us and His fire can be seen in us. Without a daily place, an altar where the fire within can be stoked hot, we walk common to the world around us.

Our lives can be up-and-down, inconsistent, unstable dramas. This book has been written to help you reflect consistently the lasting, life-transforming fire of God and be revived again. You have a role to play in this drama! Your role is to build and maintain the place inside your heart that reflects commitment to the One who created you and knows the ultimate best for you. That place is where you prepare for daily sacrifices. This is where your identity shines, and you reflect fully who you are in the time and place in history that you occupy. Our hope for the pages ahead is to remind you that you have a purpose and destiny, and to encourage you "to fan into flame the gift of God" that dwells so richly within you (2 Timothy 1:6).

God's fire is like a diamond. Diamonds sparkle with fiery reflections and refractions of light, every facet beautiful. These gemstones are solid forms of the element carbon, which is crystalized through high temperature and pressure. Their beauty reflects that bonded heat and strain, which also help determine a diamond's worth.

We will be studying the mystery of fire as it is reflected in Scripture, the Word of God, much as a diamond reflects the sparkling brilliance of light. There are eight kinds of fire we must consider—including those that Scripture warns us against—both for our spiritual well-being and for the effectiveness of our ministry in the world around us:

1. The *fire* of the Holy Spirit, the real and present indwelling of the Spirit of the Living God.
2. The *fire* of the love of God—the fire of the cross. The cross is the meeting place between heaven and earth.
3. The *fire* of God's word to us. Scripture tells us that "the grass withers, the flower fades, but the word of

our God stands forever" (Isaiah 40:8 NKJV). Having a place in our hearts ready to receive all that God will speak to us helps stabilize us for the storms of life ahead.

4. The *fire* of holiness. God's Word says, "Be holy, because I am holy" (1 Peter 1:16). God will not ask of us what we cannot attain. Not being common to the world around us is holiness.

5. The *fire* of worship and prayer. The presentation of this fire is pleasing in God's eyes and causes His favor to rest on us. This fire must be guarded diligently. We have an enemy who seeks to steal and destroy this favor.

6. The *fire* of impurity. This comes from the mixture of soul and spirit in our worship. It includes what the Lord tried to guard His people against as they moved into the Promised Land. This is called Yahwism— their worship of God among the many Canaanite gods.

7. The *fire* of hell. We will discuss how Satan builds altars so his fire can burn. He hopes to redirect the passion of God's people to himself.

8. The *fire* of ministry that reflects our call and destiny. One of the pressing needs of our age is for men and women to rise up and live in their true callings. Without consistent altars for this fire, confusion abounds and the Kingdom tarries.

The time is now! Let's build our altars so that fresh, perpetual fire burns. For too long we have let the altars of our hearts become common and lie in disarray. God's people must awaken and once more prepare places for the fire to fall. And it is not just any fire—but the fire of a Living God, the possessor of heaven and earth. The hour is late, and the days are evil. We must redeem the time. Let's restore the altars of our hearts throughout the land. If we will build, then He will come, and the fire will fall.

QUESTIONS FOR REFLECTION

1. Why must we have a generation that tears down iniquitous altars?
2. Why would an altar establish a meeting place of relationship?
3. What kind of fire do you most desire to see established (or reestablished) on your altar?

2

Fresh Fire for Salvation and Revival

When I, Chuck, was young, I attended church with my grand-mother. She always sat in the second row. I sat next to her on the pew by the center aisle. The pastor would be behind the pulpit speaking. At the end of each service, he would say to all of us, "If the Lord is speaking to you or knocking at the door of your heart, you need to come forward to the altar."

People would then go up front to the kneeling bench. Then the pastor or someone—in my mind—older and wiser would be on the other side of the bench to pray with them. At the end, those who went forward would testify how the Lord had spoken to them to know Him, or how He asked them to serve in some special way. On some occasions, people would share how they had been away from the Lord but that very day had "returned to the altar"!

What did that mean? First of all, I knew I could not go forward unless I heard the Lord speak to me, and I was not sure what He would say if He spoke. In my mind, I did think that if I was going to go to heaven, I would have to *go to the altar*. Sunday after Sunday I heard the same offer from the pastor, and I waited to see if the Lord wanted me to come. Finally, on September 11, 1963, I heard the Lord speak to me for the first time.

He said, *Today is your day. Will you come with Me? I want your heart.*

I knew I was to go to the altar.

What Is an Altar?

Mention the word *altar* in today's culture, and you are assured of a variety of responses. Some who were raised in church traditions that included altar services envision wood, carpet, a brass rail and sturdy furnishings. Others might take their cues from movie scenes where someone or something is about to be sacrificed, and the hero arrives just in time to prevent certain death. Still others might be hard-pressed for a response at all.

But what about the altar as described in the Bible—and what, if anything, does it mean for us today? The word *altar* comes from a verb that means literally "to slaughter." A dictionary definition elaborates: "an elevated place or structure . . . at which religious rites are performed or on which sacrifices are offered to gods, ancestors, etc."* Furthermore, the word *altar* is used in Hebrews 13:10 for the sacrifice offered upon it—the sacrifice Christ offered.†

When our teams travel through the world today from nation to nation on prayer journeys, one thing we instruct

---

*Dictionary.com, s.v. "altar," last modified 2020, https://www.dictionary.com/browse/altar?s=t.
†Easton, M. G., *Easton's Bible Dictionary* (New York: Harper & Brothers, 1893).

them to do is look for ancient altars. One of my memorable journeys was to the altar at Delphi. The Temple of Apollo at Delphi, as it survives, dates to the fourth century BC, but the foundation is original to an earlier version from the sixth century, which replaces an even older seventh-century version. The temple was home to the oracle of Apollo. The oracle— the Pythia or high priestess—was consulted before all major undertakings from war to the founding of colonies. She delivered messages from Apollo in the form of riddles that allowed for multiple interpretations. Some say the priestess chewed laurel leaves (sacred to Apollo) to become god-inspired.

At each of the many places of worship, our teams would repent for how the earth had been defiled. We would then renounce any known false prophecies that we could find recorded. We would then ask the Spirit of God to come and neutralize the site. We would ask that the powers and principalities that had been invoked and sacrificed to would let go of the captives that were held from knowing the one true God and Father today.

In today's culture, altars are not nearly so common, though many memorials are really altars. Probably the most recent is the memorial at the 9/11 site in New York City where the World Trade Center towers once stood. Rites and rituals will take place for years to come, remembering the lives lost on that tragic day. The current 9/11 national memorial has become a modern-day altar.

Unofficial or Home Altars

There are many unofficial altars. Usually, they are not so obvious because they are in our homes and have much to do with individualism. Home altars today may have everything from pictures of the Virgin Mary to statues of the round-bellied Buddha. Some people worship pop idols or movie stars and build altars to them. In ministering deliverance to individuals through the years, we have found that some people build inordinate altars around individual relationships.

While ministering in Malaysia, I, Chuck, crossed the street to a tailor to get a couple of shirts made. The price for clothing in Asian countries is amazing, and the quality is great. I chose the fabric, and after measurements were taken I was assured the garments would be ready the next day.

Upon returning at noon break the following day, I found the tailor sitting in front of a statue of Buddha, whom he had served rice. Incense was burning and the man was worshiping. I apologized for interrupting, but he told me that this was my only time to receive the shirts.

John Price, a ministry friend, had gone into the shop with me. I paid for the shirts and we left, but each time I wore one of them, John would remind me that they had been dedicated to idols. I eventually rid my house of the garments. Many homes have altars dedicated to worship, some to the Lord of heaven and earth, others to false gods.

While today's altars are not always obvious, they were very apparent during Bible times. Genesis 8:20 tells of Noah building "an altar to the LORD." Many Old Testament altars commonly consisted of heaps of several stones or sometimes just one large stone, since stones were plentiful. In Noah's case, he took "some of all the clean animals and clean birds" and sacrificed burnt offerings on the altar he had built. In the book of Acts we read that the apostle Paul came upon an altar with this inscription: "TO AN UNKNOWN GOD" (Acts 17:23). Like today, even in biblical times not all altars were dedicated to the one, true God.

The Covenant and the Altar

Under the Old Covenant, there was a direct correlation between obedience to God's Law and being blessed as a nation. In contrast, a curse followed when someone stepped outside of the covenant or protection of God. The book of Judges demonstrates that every time Israel disobeyed the Lord, they neglected the altar of God and let the fire go out. When the people let the fire go out on God's altar, then they usually built altars to false gods, particularly those related to Baal.

In the Old Testament, we can trace this pattern for disaster:

• Neglect of the altar
• Lack of holiness
• Lack of fear of the Lord
• Self-sufficiency

The attitude of neglect leads to false pride and the denial of God's power. It embodies the warning of 2 Timothy 3:5 against "having a form of godliness but denying its power." That was the result when God's people neglected the altar and let the fire go out. When we neglect the cross of Christ as our spiritual altar of worship and adoration, the power of His Spirit lessens and eventually departs.

For believers, the cross is not only where the price of sin has been paid but also a sign of the hope of eternal victory through the power of His resurrection. Neglecting the cross is turning our backs on the eternal hope. When we neglect the altar of the cross, we have nothing but the form of religion without the life, power, love or fruit of the Holy Spirit.

A Place of Relationship

The altar is a place of relationship between God and us—a place of pure and wholehearted relationship where our Holy God can meet with us and His fire can fall. God created us for relationship with Him and those around us. This relationship is best demonstrated by giving and receiving: "God so loved the world that he gave his one and only Son, that whoever believes in him shall not perish but have eternal life" (John 3:16).

The altar was established so His people could be restored to fellowship with Him by bringing sin, guilt and fellowship offerings. In God's plan, the altar is the central place for the expression of lasting love. This is why the altar is needed; at the altar we give and receive. For us, the altar is the place of receiving everything God has for us. The altar stood at the core of God's plan of salvation because it pointed to the cross of Christ, which is the source of all God's blessings.

In the Old Testament, the altar was directly related to the spiritual and material blessings God intended for His people. Exodus 23:25–26 offers this promise from God: "Worship the LORD your God, and his blessing will be on your food and water. I will take away sickness from among you, and none will miscarry or be barren in your land. I will give you a full life span."

Furthermore, Exodus 20:24 records that when God talked with the Israelites in the wilderness, He said: "Make an altar of earth for me and sacrifice on it your burnt offerings and fellowship offerings, your sheep and goats and your cattle. Wherever I cause my name to be honored, I will come to you and bless you."

In this book, we are not talking about a literal altar made of stone or physical sacrifices. We are talking about the spiritual implications of the altar for our daily lives and walks—implications that can enhance our spiritual growth, make the victorious Christian life a reality, glorify the risen Lord, as well as release revival fire for spiritual awakening and renewal.

Restoring the Altar: What It Means

Restoring the altar for fresh fire today is not about building a physical altar or maintaining a natural fire. Remember, the altar God desires is a heart that is fully committed to Him. For God's people today, building and restoring the spiritual altar to house the spiritual fire of revival in God's Kingdom is far more important. Remember, the Old Testament altar was simply a foreshadowing of what was to come through Christ Jesus.

Restoring the spiritual altar today provides the foundation for renewing our:

- Love for God
- Dedication to God
- Fellowship with God
- Relationship with others
- Prayer
- Blessings from God—salvation, healing, fruits of the Holy Spirit, power, anointing, victory, provision
- Covenant to live a life of true obedience to glorify God by living only for Him
- Commitment to a true revival
- Worship

The altar is where worship of God almighty originates. Worship is acknowledging God as Creator and Redeemer, the beginning and the end. We not only make Him first, but also start everything and finish everything for Him and with Him. When He is at the beginning of everything, that is the beginning of our:

- Life
- Desire
- Ambition
- Vision
- Mission
- Dreams
- Will
- Plan
- Purpose
- Decisions
- Determination
- Talent
- Family
- Relatives
- Friends
- Ministry
- Business
- Profession
- Success
- Accomplishments
- Fame
- Future
- Time
- Day
- Year
- Season

Yes, worship is placing God first in everything we are and do: "Honor the LORD with your possessions, and with the firstfruits of all your increase" (Proverbs 3:9 NKJV). This can be done, however, only in the context of a right-standing relationship with God. Right relationship with God is the result of loving God with all our hearts, souls, minds and strength; accepting and submitting to His authority fully; and walking in the holy reverence of His majesty. The only way we can build an altar and bring the sacrifice of worship that honors God is by making Him Lord of everything. When we start living by the principles of His power and authority, it becomes very natural and desirable to be in right standing with the One we worship.

Keeping the Altar Pure

Without an altar of worship, spiritual progress and lasting change are not possible. That is the reason why God reviews altar worship at the beginning of new movements. Take, for example, how He dealt with Adam's offspring. The first thing God checked was to find out if Cain and Abel had prepared acceptable sacrifices of worship. Both Cain and Abel brought their offerings; however, the Lord looked at both and did not accept Cain's offering. Cain wanted to worship the Lord the way he chose, while Abel was obedient to revelation they had received from God about an offering of worship—which likely was placed on some type of altar.

The issue was not so much what they brought or what they did, but why they brought it and how they did it. Cain worshiped the way he chose. The Lord warned him, but he refused to listen to God or obey Him. Yes, obedience is much better than sacrifice. When a person chooses his or her own way to worship, the door is open to the enemy.

That was what happened to Cain. In spite of the Lord's warning that "sin was crouching at [his] door," Cain hardened his heart and refused to listen (Genesis 4:7). He killed his brother, and it would not be hard to imagine he did it with the same knife that Abel had used to sacrifice the animals he had brought for worship. If so, and if Abel had constructed some type of altar for his offering, would it not be amazing that the first murder was related to an altar of worship? We do not know this for sure. But we do know that when an altar of worship is corrupted, it affects our spiritual sensitivity to hear and obey God.

At the beginning of the New Testament Church, there was a similar situation. Husband and wife, Ananias and Sapphira, sold a piece of property and brought some of the money to the apostles for distribution to those who had need. Others, who sold their property, brought everything and gave a true accounting when they placed the money at the apostles' feet. Ananias and Sapphira kept part of the money, but they pretended as if they had brought all of it.

Peter saw through their deception. "Peter said, 'Ananias, how is it that Satan has so filled your heart that you have lied to the Holy Spirit . . . ?'" (Acts 5:3). Like Cain, this couple decided to worship the Lord the way they wanted. That opened the doors of their hearts to evil: "How is it that Satan has so filled your heart?" They lied to the Holy Spirit in agreement with Satan and engaged with their full will with evil. As a result, they came under the judgment of God.

How do we keep the altar pure? There are three key elements:

1. The first key element in keeping the altar of worship pure is to approach God in holy reverence and according to His Word.

   Even David made a mistake by not following the instructions of God when he brought the Ark of the Covenant to Jerusalem on a cart. In spite of the great worship and celebration, he was not acting in accordance with God's directives. "The LORD's anger burned against Uzzah, and he struck him down because he had put his hand on the ark. So he died there before God" (1 Chronicles 13:10).

The Word of God gives us clear guidance on how to approach Him: "Let us then approach the throne of grace with confidence, so that we may receive mercy and find grace to help us in our time of need" (Hebrews 4:16).

2. The second key element in keeping the altar of worship pure is to build or renew an altar of worship at the beginning of every new season or change God brings into our lives.

   This builds a solid foundation for what is coming, or for where the Lord is taking us.

   The first person the Bible records who built an altar for God was Noah. The Lord looked for someone who would build an ark so that He could save the generation. He found Noah: "By faith Noah, when warned about things not yet seen, in holy fear built an ark to save his family. By his faith he condemned the world and became heir of the righteousness that comes by faith" (Hebrews 11:7).

   After the flood destroyed everything, the Lord told Noah to come out of the ark and start anew. As soon as Noah came off the ark with his family and the animals to start a new season, he built an altar. "Then Noah built an altar to the LORD and, taking some of all the clean animals and clean birds, he sacrificed burnt offerings on it" (Genesis 8:20).

   As a result of Noah's offering, the Lord responded in three ways:

   • He was very pleased with the aroma of the sacrifice of obedience.

- He promised not to destroy the earth by flood again and promised the seasons to mankind.
- He blessed Noah and his family and told them to be fruitful on the earth.

Abraham, the father of faith, also stepped into a new season by building an altar. He had accepted the call of God to leave his country, his people and his father's household to follow God. When he arrived in the land of the Canaanites, the Lord appeared to him and promised the land to Abraham's offspring. "So he [Abraham] built an altar there to the LORD who had appeared to him" (Genesis 12:7).

From the beginning of that new season on, one of the marks of Abraham's life was building altars to the Lord. The most important altar Abraham built was the one on Mount Moriah to sacrifice Isaac, his son, in obedience to the voice of God. At that altar Abraham received divine approval as well as eternal promises from God about his descendants (see Genesis 22:15–18).

3. The third key element in keeping the altar of worship pure is a foundation of true spiritual awakening or reformation beginning with restoration of the altar.

   Joshua and Zerubbabel started a reformation process by rebuilding the altar of the Lord. They "began to build the altar of the God of Israel to sacrifice burnt offerings on it. . . . Despite their fear of the peoples around them, they built the altar on its foundation" (Ezra 3:2–3). Building the altar on the old foundation signified that they were committed to securing the presence of God through worship.

The rebuilding of the altar for worship reestablished their relationship with God. Scripture is clear about this commitment: "Love the Lord your God with all your heart and with all your soul and with all your mind and with all your strength" (Mark 12:30). There cannot be a true and lasting reformation for awakening without the altar of worship. Rebuilding the altar of worship is a sign of commitment to "seek first his kingdom and his righteousness" (Matthew 6:33).

At the Altar

The worship of God is the foundation for all the blessings He has for His people (see Exodus 20:24). We receive God's blessings and become blessings through worship. His blessings are released through our obedience. God's mandate to start reformation is by rebuilding the altar for His presence so that He can bless us with courage, wisdom, power, strength, guidance, protection and provision.

I, Chuck, wrote these words of definition in *Worship As It Is in Heaven* and want to share them with you here:

A major shift is coming in the way we worship and acknowledge God. . . . God is saying that in the times of drought and crisis that will manifest in the days ahead, we will lead His people to:

- Worship expressly on a daily basis. There is coming a Holy Spirit movement in us and around us. We will sing songs of breakthrough. We will shout our way into victory. We will dance in ways we have never danced. We will prostrate ourselves as Hannah lay before the altar, and more.

- Give incredibly. Incredible giving is linked with miraculous and demonstrative acts of faith. . . .
- Be strategically creative. This creativity is stored within us. Most of us are not aware of how deep God's well really goes. This creativity will be used over our mission and assignment. He will show us daily how to advance creatively in our mission.*

We worship so that we might "know Christ and the power of his resurrection" (Philippians 3:10). At the altar we show our devotion. Let's turn now to understanding just what an altar is.

*John Dickson and Chuck D. Pierce, *Worship As It Is in Heaven* (Minneapolis: Chosen, 2010), 42.

QUESTIONS FOR REFLECTION

1. What is an altar for you?
2. Why is understanding covenant so important for flaming revival fire?
3. Describe ways you can keep your altar pure in order to have an extraordinary relationship with Lord.

3

What Is the Altar of God?

When I, Chuck, came to the Lord and began to seek Him on a daily basis, I became aware of two things: how much I needed Him, and how powerful He was to answer prayer. I remember seeking Him over a severe situation that had entered my life. I knew that the situation was beyond me, and only through His intervening could change come.

He spoke to me one morning and said, *Get this on My altar.*

I realized how much fretting and begging instead of faith praying I was doing. He then showed me that if I truly got the situation on His altar, He was free to do three things: *keep, kill or change* what I was carrying in my heart.

A Place of Divine Encounter

The altar of God is a place of divine encounter through the cross of Christ. The altar of God is where we receive mercy and grace for salvation. This is where we align with the power of the Holy Spirit for sonship and worship. The altar of God is where we enter into His holy presence for everlasting covenant and ongoing renewal of life. This causes us to reflect His glory as we are being transformed into the image of Christ.

The altar of God is a place of moment-by-moment surrender of one's will in order to encounter God. Only one with a sacrificed will dwells together in harmony with Him. "It is no longer I who live, but Christ lives in me" (Galatians 2:20 NKJV), and "I die daily" (1 Corinthians 15:31 NKJV). The altar is the place where we offer our whole lives to God. Paul directs us to "offer your bodies as a living sacrifice" (Romans 12:1). It is no longer our will or interest that matters; everything we have and are belongs to Jesus. Until we come to the altar (place of sacrifice) and give our fully submitted lives, Jesus Christ has not become our Lord and King (see Romans 14:7), whom we serve daily.

The Christian life should be a life where Christ lives in us. Just as Jesus said as He placed His life on the Father's altar to bring the redemptive plan into fullness in the earth realm, so we say: "Father . . . not my will, but yours be done" (Luke 22:42). Staying at the altar, for a believer, is dwelling in holy covenant communion with the Living God and living a lifestyle of obedience. We become, therefore, a living sacrifice.

As we study the Old Testament, we discover three types of altars. A basic understanding of these three types is necessary in order to restore our altars for fresh fire.

The Altar of Stone

The first type of altar we find in the Old Testament was made of rocks or dirt set on high places or a hill. This kind of altar did not have any particular shape or specified location and was used to burn sacrifices or offerings to God.

As we have noted, the first time an altar is mentioned is when Noah built an altar to the Lord after the Great Flood. Then he took "some of all the clean animals and clean birds, [and] he sacrificed burnt offerings on it" (Genesis 8:20). The Word says that the Lord was pleased with Noah's offering. Later on, we find Abraham building a similar type of altar. (Genesis 12–13 and 22 offer examples of this.) Clearly, God accepted such altars. Psalm 51:17 explains that God is interested in the shape of the heart, not the shape of the altar: "My sacrifice is a humble spirit, O God; you will not reject a humble and repentant heart" (GNT).

Another important aspect of this first type of altar is that there is no mention of a priest. It seems that the presence of a priest was unnecessary (see Exodus 20:24–26). This altar type was between God and the individual(s) who had a desire to worship and honor Him.

For today's New Testament believers, this point is crucial. Our individual altars are very important to God, and He enjoys it when we gather together to worship and honor Him. He promises to be there, as Jesus stated.

The private altar must be preceded by a personal or private life of worship, studying the Word and honoring God with everything we have and do. If we do not have a personal altar where we bring sacrifices, praises and adoration to God in private, the public altar will not impress God in the least. Public activity, performance or even ministry will never replace a personal relationship with God. We can only minister to others in His name when we take seriously our private ministry to Him as His children. We must, therefore, first restore:

- Our personal altars where we as individuals bring sacrifices of praise and worship
- Our family altars where a family comes together to honor and glorify God
- Our ministry altars where people in a ministry gather to fulfill His eternal purpose and will

The Altar of Bronze

The second type of altar in the Old Testament, the bronze altar, had a specific shape and location. The first bronze altar to be used for sacrifices was built according to God's detailed pattern and placed at the entrance to the Tabernacle. Later one was built for the entrance to Solomon's Temple. When the work of constructing both the Tabernacle and Temple was finally completed, and God's specific instructions had been followed by the priests and people regarding burnt offerings, His glory came and filled the Tabernacle and the Temple, and His fire fell to consume the sacrifices placed there (see Exodus 27; 40; Leviticus 9:24; 2 Chronicles 4–5; 7).

Look at this vivid description:

When Solomon finished praying, fire came down from heaven and consumed the burnt offering and the sacrifices, and the glory of the LORD filled the temple. The priests could not enter the temple of the LORD because the glory of the LORD filled it. When all the Israelites saw the fire coming down and the glory of the LORD above the temple, they knelt on the pavement with their faces to the ground, and they worshiped and gave thanks to the LORD, saying, "He is good; his love endures forever."

2 Chronicles 7:1–3

The glory and fire of God were the result of building according to code—God's code. Whenever the divine pattern is neglected or replaced by human methods and assumptions, there is neither glory nor fire. What we do have is religion without power, and activities without lasting impact. Do we not need both today? Both the glory *and* the fire of God in our lives, churches and work?

How can we be sure that the altar is built according to God's pattern? The foundation of the altar in the New Testament has been firmly established upon the sacrificial redemptive work of Christ Jesus, and no further embellishment of this altar is needed.

As Paul states,

> By the grace God has given me, I laid a foundation as an expert builder, and someone else is building on it. But each one should be careful how he builds. For no one can lay any foundation other than the one already laid, which is Jesus Christ. If any man builds on this foundation using gold, silver, costly stones, wood, hay or straw, his work will be shown for what it is, because the Day will bring it to light. It will be revealed with fire, and the fire will test the quality of each man's work. If what he has built survives, he will receive his reward. If it is burned up, he will suffer loss; he himself will be saved, but only as one escaping through the flames.
>
> 1 Corinthians 3:10–15

The Altar of Gold

The third type of altar is the gold altar of incense. Like the bronze altar, it was built with a specific pattern and purpose, but it was placed inside the Tabernacle and the Temple (see Exodus 30:1–10; 40:26; 1 Kings 7:48; Revelation 5:8;

8:3–5). Rather than being used for sin or guilt offerings, this altar was exclusively for burning incense for the purpose of worship. It was placed in front of the curtain or veil separating the Holy Place from the Most Holy Place; in other words, the last thing before entrance into the Holy of Holies was the altar of incense.

The altar of incense is all about worship: raising the sweet aroma of praise. We can enter into His holy presence only through true worship. Worship is the closest thing to the heart of God. In fact, the only thing we can offer God directly in this life is worship. Only God is worthy of worship and adoration.

Another name for this golden altar was the "altar of fragrant incense" (Leviticus 4:7). This name gives us an additional facet of worship—prayer. Whether we offer intercession or humble appeal, God desires to hear our prayers.

If we cry to God, He will answer us and show us great and mighty things. King David stated this truth: "O You who hear prayer, to You all flesh will come" (Psalm 65:2 NKJV). "The LORD is far from the wicked, but he hears the prayer of the righteous" (Proverbs 15:29).

There Is a Blueprint!

The concept of the altar, to worship the God of Abraham, Isaac and Jacob, was originated by God Himself, who desires sincere worship in spirit and in truth. That is why He called Moses to the mountain and gave him an exact blueprint. God gave him specific instructions with warning not to change any of the plans for the altar, the location of the altar and, most importantly, the purpose of the altar.

Following God's desire with total obedience is what makes worship relational and meaningful. Samuel told King Saul: "Does the LORD delight in burnt offerings and sacrifices as much as in obeying the voice of the LORD? To obey is better than sacrifice, and to heed is better than the fat of rams" (1 Samuel 15:22).

Divine Plan for the Altar

We need to understand and follow the divine plan for the altar that will allow God's glory to come and fill our lives, churches and ministries. The divine plan is found in the cross of Christ. God is committed to exalting the cross of His Son. A true fire of revival and manifestation of God's glory, therefore, demands our return to living by, and preaching, the cross of Christ in its simplicity:

> For the message of the cross is foolishness to those who are perishing, but to us who are being saved it is the power of God. For it is written, "I will destroy the wisdom of the wise; the intelligence of the intelligent I will frustrate." . . . God was pleased through the foolishness of what was preached to save those who believe. Jews demand miraculous signs and Greeks look for wisdom, but we preach Christ crucified: a stumbling block to Jews and foolishness to Gentiles, but to those whom God has called, both Jews and Greeks, Christ the power of God and the wisdom of God. For the foolishness of God is wiser than man's wisdom, and the weakness of God is stronger than man's strength. . . . It is because of him that you are in Christ Jesus, who has become for us wisdom from God—that is, our righteousness, holiness and redemption.
>
> 1 Corinthians 1:18–19, 21–25, 30

The Place of the Altar

It is important to notice where the bronze altar—also called "the altar of God" (Psalm 43:4) and "altar of the LORD" (Leviticus 17:6)—was placed: at the entrance to the Holy Place of the Tabernacle and the Temple. The priests who entered the Holy Place passed by the altar, where the sin offerings were made.

If we truly want the fire of lasting revival, we should put the cross of Christ at the entrance of every spiritual undertaking, including our church services, prayer meetings, home Bible studies and all other kinds of Christian ministries. When we come by the altar—the cross of Christ—we deal with sin; we do not entertain sin in our hearts. The altar of bronze is the place of judgment: "If we would examine ourselves first, we would not come under God's judgment" (1 Corinthians 11:31 GNT). We must examine ourselves every day as we pass by the altar into the Holy Place. Avoiding this daily discipline results in dousing the fires of revival; we reveal our childishness concerning the altar, the cross of Christ. Spiritual shortcuts are the enemy of the Holy Spirit's fire.

The Purpose of the Altar

Realizing the true purpose of the altar frees us from any fear of being what God wants us to be. God's declaration to us is truly liberating. He says to us, "The work to cover your sin and restore our relationship is done. You don't have to perform; just accept My grace."

We do not have to struggle to serve. We simply need to pass by the altar (the cross), recognizing that the debt for our sin has been paid. We do not have to labor as prisoners of condemnation: "There is now no condemnation for those who are in Christ Jesus" (Romans 8:1). The purpose of the altar is to reassure us that because we have received, now we can give to Him. When we pass by the altar into our callings, therefore, whatever those callings might be, we do everything for the glory of God. We live for Him because of what He has done for us. We serve Him out of our love for Him. As Paul wrote: "Christ's love compels us, because we are convinced that one died for all, and therefore all died. And he died for all, that those who live should no longer live for themselves but for him who died for them and was raised again" (2 Corinthians 5:14–15).

The Fire of the Altar

The fire of God in heaven is never extinguished. Sometimes in the earth, we dampen or quench that which should remain burning. Why is it important to keep the fire of God burning at all times on the altar? This was one very important warning Moses gave the Israelites after they had built the Tabernacle: "The fire must be kept burning on the altar continuously; it must not go out" (Leviticus 6:13). Without the altar there is no place for sacrifice, and without the sacrifice there is no fire. The fire of God consumes the sacrifice. Without the fire of His presence there is no glory.

So let's take a look at what happens when that fire dies and the presence of God is not real:

- *Grace becomes law, and we lose the essence of true worship.* Without God's fire burning, there is no grace to serve.
- *Responsibilities become privileges.* When the fire dies, we misuse responsibilities.

45

- *Authority becomes abusive.* We lose the compassion of God.
- *Love becomes self-serving.* We love others for wrong motives. We say we love God, but only for selfish reasons.
- *Worship becomes a ritual.* Worship loses the manifestation of the reality and presence of the Lord Jesus by the power of the Holy Spirit.
- *Ministry becomes work, an opportunity to earn a living or a chance to display our positions.* There is nothing wrong with earning a living for our daily needs. But when we focus on this, and it becomes the purpose of our ministry, we miss the point.
- *Spiritual life becomes religion.* Instead of living by faith, we practice religion.
- *Righteousness becomes an external covering for a lack of internal purity or integrity.* Outward expressions become pharisaical.
- *Spiritual gifts are used for self-glorification.* Spiritual gifts are meant to glorify the Lord Jesus Christ, not ourselves.
- *Material possessions become the most important thing in life.* Wealth becomes an end in itself with no relation to the Kingdom of God.
- *Competition becomes a lifestyle at the expense of unity in the Spirit.* We compare ourselves to others instead of to Jesus.
- *Devotion to God and dedication to God's Kingdom become the domain of "a few fanatics" instead of the lifestyle for every believer.* In order truly to say

Hallowed be Your name, we need to keep the fire of worship alive!

- *Forms of religion and activities replace our relationship with God.* God's desire is for us to move into an extraordinary relationship with Him. Form without substance cannot be allowed to replace the inner beauty of our daily relationship with our God. Otherwise, we have only a hollow, external walk— that "form of godliness" with no power.

We must protect our relationships with the Father through the Son and by the Spirit. We must protect our hearts and consciences so we "see" God. We must protect our place of meeting—the altar—where we come to the Lord.

QUESTIONS FOR REFLECTION

1. What is your own working definition of *altar*?
2. Describe restoration of the altar and its importance, in your own words.
3. What do you think might change in your local fellowship if the altar there was restored?

4

Protecting the Altar from Ruin

I, Chuck, love to travel from nation to nation. Alemu also travels internationally each year, and we both share a heart for the nations. In America, I have been honored to travel from state to state and region to region gathering God's intercessory watchman remnant.

Recently, we were in New Jersey with John and Sheryl Price for a major gathering called "Rebuilding the Altar of Our Nation." We had state representatives from each of America's original thirteen colonies, the colonies that formed the root of righteousness in this nation. Additionally, Nova Scotia, which once was considered for possible statehood, had a delegation of leaders and intercessors at this gathering. The purpose for meeting was to restore an altar of worship to the Living God, who sacrificed His Son for the redemption of all people in every nation. This meeting was historical and key for the future of America.

While I was in New Jersey, I went to Basking Ridge to be with Peter and Trisha Roselle, who are pastors of the wonderful apostolic King of Kings Worship Center. In preparation for the "thirteen colony" meeting that I described above, they had been teaching their people on the topic of "Restoring the Altar." Trisha shared the following with us:

Protecting your personal altar is foundational for an ongoing relationship with our Creator and Redeemer. We protect the significance of our place and vision. We must keep gaining understanding and adjusting strategy so as not to lose the original purpose, value or intent of the Lord's visitation and redemptive plan. Building an altar is to worship God as a point of contact over His original plan and is very important.

When Moses was on the mountain, he received detailed plans to build the altar of God as a part of the Tabernacle of worship. God wanted to dwell among His people, the Israelites. "Then have them make a sanctuary for me, and I will dwell among them. Make this tabernacle and all its furnishings exactly like the pattern I will show you" (Exodus 25:8–9). Their responsibility was hosting the presence of the Lord who came to dwell among them. We preserve this altar to enhance our personal relationship with Him. In the Old Testament, we see the importance of the altar, the maintenance and what happens when we neglect or misappropriate our responsibility.

Every true restoration started with the rebuilding of the altar of God. When God's remaining people came back from Babylon, the first thing they did was rebuild the altar of God. To make this permanent, they laid the foundation of the Temple and restored the blessings of God to the nation.

The Lord said to them,

"From this day on, from this twenty-fourth day
of the ninth month, give careful thought to the day

when the foundation of the LORD's temple was
laid. Give careful thought: Is there yet any seed left
in the barn? Until now, the vine and the fig tree,
the pomegranate and the olive tree have not borne
fruit. 'From this day on I will bless you.'"

Haggai 2:18–19

Therefore, the blessing of the people of covenant related
directly to their life of worship and devotion to God.

Eli was both high priest and one of the last judges of
ancient Israel before the rule of the kings began. His two
sons were corrupt, degrading the priesthood, and the Lord
admonished Eli with these words: "Why do you scorn my
sacrifice and offering that I prescribed for my dwelling?
Why do you honor your sons more than me by fattening
yourselves on the choice parts of every offering made by
my people Israel?" (1 Samuel 2:29). Eli failed to restrain his
sons for their blasphemous behavior, and the Lord spoke
again to Eli through the young boy Samuel. Instead of repenting and making right his relationship with the Lord, Eli
responded, "He is the LORD; let him do what is good in his
eyes" (1 Samuel 3:18).

As a result, Israel was defeated by their enemies. The
Ark of the Lord was captured by the Philistines. Eli's sons
were killed. The protection of God was removed, and the
high priest died. Eli's daughter-in-law was pregnant and gave
birth to a son whom she named Ichabod, saying, "'The glory
has departed from Israel'—because of the capture of the ark
of God and the deaths of her father-in-law and her husband"
(1 Samuel 4:21).

The saddest thing was that the base treatment of the altar
of God affected the identity of the new generation: They
became a generation without the glory of His presence. Furthermore, the Lord destroyed their false altars. "Their heart
is deceitful, and now they must bear their guilt. The LORD

will demolish their altars and destroy their sacred stones" (Hosea 10:2).

The altar is equally important today, and our treatment of it equally affects our lives. In future chapters we will discuss the blessing of maintaining the altar. Now, let's take a look at how we ruin the altar of God.

Ruining the Altar of God

As we see from accounts in Scripture, the altar was ruined when the priests, prophets and spiritual leaders stopped caring for, neglected or misused it. Here are ten specific ways that an altar can be ruined:

1. Not Protecting the Place of Sacrifice

The ruin of the altar of God probably occurs most often because of neglect: We are busy attending to our personal interests. This was true in the time of Haggai the prophet. Those who had come back from captivity to rebuild the Temple of God became preoccupied with building their own houses. Nothing was wrong with building their own homes, but in doing so they neglected the house of God. The Lord sent three prophets—Haggai, Zechariah and Malachi—to challenge the people to build and maintain the Temple.

The same thing is true today in our personal lives and ministries. If we want the fire of true revival, we must do as Jesus said: "Seek first his kingdom and his righteousness, and all these things will be given to you as well" (Matthew 6:33).

The Lord's altar is being ruined in individual lives, churches and ministries where we have made personal interest and financial gain priorities. We need to go back to our original calling, restore our altars and ask God to send His fire. Only then will the nations see His fire and return to Him, crying out, "The LORD—he is God! The LORD—he is God!" (1 Kings 18:39 NKJV).

2. *Lack of Concern for the Things of the Lord*

One serious sin of the Pharisees during the time of Jesus' earthly ministry was that they did not care about the things of the Lord. They were more concerned about their traditions. They did not practice sincere worship of God in truth and in the Spirit. Because of this attitude, they ruined the altar of God.

This is also true today, both on a personal level and on the church or ministry level. Many times, as human beings, we let Kingdom values and issues take a backseat to our traditions, cultures, practices, paradigms, worldviews, policies and social status. When human concerns take precedence over Kingdom values, the altar is broken and needs to be restored through repentance.

3. *Building an Altar for False Gods*

The worship of false gods was one of the main sins of God's people in the Old Testament and caused great ruin. Every time we exalt persons, spiritual gifts, programs or activities above the things of God, we ruin His altar. This happens because we give to these false altars, whatever they might be, what belongs to God alone. Our God does not share His glory.

Even in Christianity we raise up heroes and superstars. In God's Kingdom, however, there is no such thing; all of us are equally valuable parts of one Body. When we attempt to lift ourselves or others into glorifying roles, we must turn and repent and give glory and praise to the only One who deserves it. For revival fire to burn continuously, our hearts must turn fully to God.

4. Not Bringing the Right Sacrifice

We read in the Old Testament that the people violated God's Word when they brought unacceptable sacrifices. Unacceptable sacrifices ruined the altar of worship. We do that many times during our personal, family and church worship times when we fail to bring God the best; the best of our time, gifts and attention.

In 1 Chronicles 28:9–10, we read the stern instructions King David gave to his young son Solomon, who was chosen to build the Temple. This passage is applicable to every child of God who desires to please Him through right sacrifices of service and obedience. It calls us to:

- Acknowledge the God of our fathers
- Serve Him with wholehearted devotion
- Serve Him with a willing mind
- Know that the Lord searches every heart and understands every motive behind our thoughts
- Seek Him, for He will be found
- Be strong and courageous
- Remember that God will not fail or forsake us
- Do the work

Whenever we are committed to bringing a true sacrifice in total obedience, there will always be challenges. These promises given to Solomon are an encouragement for us.

5. Defiling the Altar by the Sin of Selfishness

Selfishness and greed defile the altar of true worship and adoration. This point is clearly illustrated in 1 Samuel 2 by the wicked lifestyle of the sons of Eli the priest. They did not honor the Lord with the sacrifices the people brought; they were simply interested in taking the best for themselves. They used force to take meat intended for the altar, scorning the ordained pattern for the portions the priests were to receive. The Bible describes them this way: "Eli's sons were wicked men; they had no regard for the LORD. . . . This sin of the young men was very great in the LORD's sight, for they were treating the LORD's offering with contempt" (1 Samuel 2:12, 17).

This example is extreme, but whenever a person puts his selfish interest before the glory or purpose of God, the result is the same: God's altar is defiled. True restoration is needed, and needed fast, before the glory departs and the Lord removes individuals who treat the altar of worship with contempt.

We might say, "That was just in the Old Testament." But remember Ananias and Sapphira: Because of their love of money they lied to the Holy Spirit and died on the spot. When selfishness defiles the altar, it is a very serious matter, and, sadly, this is going on in the lives of individuals as well as in churches and ministries. It is time to restore the altar so God's fire and glory can return to us.

6. Offering Sacrifice for the Wrong Reason

King Saul lost his kingship because he offered sacrifices he was not authorized to make. When he saw his soldiers begin to scatter in the face of war with the Philistines, rather than wait for Samuel to arrive he made an offering in panic. The prophet Samuel rebuked Saul for this: "What have you done? . . . You acted foolishly. . . . Your kingdom will not endure" (1 Samuel 13:11, 13–14).

Fear and unbelief are enemies of true worship; we cannot worship until we start trusting God. How many times have we acted like Saul in our worship and devotional times? Because of our commitment to our own agendas, we decide we cannot wait any longer. God has not shown up on our timetable; therefore, we determine to move on. In reality, it is not moving *on* but moving *out* of what God would like to do on His timetable. Let us not move out from where God wants to move us because of our lack of patience or our preplanned agenda.

7. Offering Sacrifice Out of a Prideful Heart

Probably the best example of a prideful heart is King Uzziah, who took it upon himself to burn incense on the altar within the Holy Place.

As a young ruler, King Uzziah started right. He had no experience or training to lead as a king, but he did have the wisdom to seek help from a prophet named Zechariah. Zechariah taught Uzziah the one crucial tactic for success as a king: the fear of the Lord. Scripture says that "as long as he sought the LORD, God gave him success" (2 Chronicles 26:5). That is, as long as Uzziah realized the limitations of his experience, knowledge, wisdom and natural resources in the context of God's resources, he was successful.

But then, "when King Uzziah became strong, he grew arrogant" (2 Chronicles 26:16 GNT):

His fame spread far and wide, for he was greatly helped until he became powerful. But after Uzziah became powerful, his

56

pride led to his downfall. He was unfaithful to the LORD his God, and entered the temple of the LORD to burn incense on the altar of incense.

2 Chronicles 26:15–16

There are several valuable lessons we can learn from King Uzziah's fall from favor because of his pride:

FEAR OF THE LORD

As long as Uzziah walked in the fear of the Lord, he gave priority to the voice of God, trusting the message of the prophet of God who understood the visions and revelation of God. Uzziah recognized his need for spiritual covering and accountability. The fear of the Lord is indeed the beginning of wisdom; as well as knowledge, understanding, discernment, true worship, relationship, fulfillment, obedience, success, impact and effectiveness.

SEEKING THE LORD

Scripture says that Uzziah was successful as long as he sought the Lord. Seeking the Lord is a desire to know God and to fellowship with Him. It is chasing after God, holding on to Him, obeying His purpose and honoring Him. Seeking the Lord leads to true worship—individually, within families, and in a church or ministry context. For many of us, this may be the missing piece we have been longing for.

SUCCESS IN THE LORD

Because of King Uzziah's fear of the Lord and commitment to seeking Him, God gave him great success in war, in building towns and cities, in constructing a water system and in developing a flourishing agricultural economy. Success is a gift based on the favor of God. When God brings success, He gives us power to exceed expectations and surpass existing standards.

FAILURE THROUGH PRIDE

Because of his success and fame, Uzziah became powerful. Sadly, this led to arrogance and pride. Uzziah not only stopped fearing and seeking the Lord, but he also defied God by burning an offering of incense without being authorized to do so. Pride defiles true worship.

The pride that brought about Uzziah's downfall made him deaf to the voice of God. It took away the holy fear of God from his heart. Uzziah's actions brought humiliation, an incurable disease (leprosy), isolation and death. Furthermore, he hindered the glory of God from being revealed to the people of God. The glory came back only after he died (see Isaiah 6:1–2).

8. Offering Sacrifice with an Insincere Heart

We cannot offer true worship, praise and thanksgiving to God while we entertain sin. Nor can we come into His presence to worship or minister with a cold heart or with the intent to impress others. This is what Jesus called worshiping in vain: "You hypocrites! Isaiah was right when he prophesied about you: 'These people honor me with their lips, but their hearts are far from me. They worship me in vain; their teachings are but rules taught by men'" (Matthew 15:8–9). When we try to worship with insincere motives, it is time to restore the altar.

9. *Offering Unauthorized Fire*

God does not allow us to bring our own fire. We may try to supply our own fire because of excitement for a ministry or because of a lack of understanding of God's will or because of impatience with God's timing. But only God's fire gives enduring results.

Our responsibility is to bring our lives as living sacrifices and put ourselves on the altar in total surrender to His will. God is the one who sends the fire. Becoming too anxious for a move of God is a serious sin against Him. The two sons of Aaron brought unauthorized fire to the altar of God. Even though they were the second generation of priests, the Lord killed them. False fire is the enemy of true spiritual revival. It works against the fire of God and the plan of God. When false fire is on the altar in the form of worship or ministry, it is time to restore the altar and consecrate it again.

10. *Offering Partial or Incomplete Sacrifice*

The cross of Christ represented and fulfilled all the sacrifices God required for sin. Christ's sacrifice was perfect and complete. As we worship God, we should include each of these Old Testament types of offerings in our worship, recognizing that the sacrificial work of Christ is what makes them pleasing and acceptable to God.

SIN OFFERING

The sin offering was made for sin that was committed unintentionally, in ignorance or in weakness. For this sin, the high priest made atonement through a sacrifice. Our High Priest, the Lord Jesus Christ, made atonement for us on the cross. But we must come to Him and ask Him to cleanse us from any hidden sin and to purify us. When we come to fellowship and worship, we must give Him permission, as David did, and say, "Search me, O God, and know my heart; test me and know my anxious thoughts. Point out anything in me that offends you, and lead me along the path of everlasting life" (Psalm 139:23–24 NLT).

GUILT OFFERING

Those who were guilty of sin or injury for which full restitution could be made gave a guilt offering. Through Christ and because of His sacrifice on the cross, we can repent and ask God for forgiveness. By God's grace that is active in our lives, we can also ask the person we offended for forgiveness. The Word of God makes this abundantly clear:

> "If you are offering your gift at the altar and there remember that your brother has something against you, leave your gift there in front of the altar. First go and be reconciled to your brother; then come and offer your gift."
>
> Matthew 5:23–24

FELLOWSHIP OFFERING

The fellowship offering was an expression of thanksgiving, covenant, celebration, peace and reconciliation. This is "coming into His gates" with thanksgiving and gratitude. Only because of Christ's sacrifice is it possible for us to be accepted and welcome in God's presence as we bring our thanksgiving to His throne.

GRAIN OFFERING

The fruit of personal labor was presented to God as an act of worship through the grain offering. This is our worship through tithes, firstfruits and service that helps to advance God's Kingdom. But the fruit of our labor finds favor and is pleasing to God only because of Christ and His sacrifice.

BURNT OFFERING

The words *burnt offering* mean literally "that which goes up to God." The entire offering (of a perfect animal without any defect) was burned to signify total dedication, complete consecration and an expression of devotion and surrender to God. It was a voluntary act, and forgiveness was involved in this offering before true worship could occur.

We must remember that only through Christ and His perfect sacrifice are we made perfect enough in the sight of God to offer ourselves to Him. Paul summarized this for the believers in Rome: "So then, my friends, because of God's great mercy to us I appeal to you: Offer yourselves as a living sacrifice to God, dedicated to his service and pleasing to him. This is the true worship that you should offer" (Romans 12:1 GNT).

Our true worship, in order not to be partial or incomplete, should include each of the five offerings above. When any one of these offerings is missing from our worship, our worship is incomplete, and it is time to restore the altar for a fresh fire of revival.

Is Your Altar Ready for Repair?

How is your altar? Have you stopped caring for it? Has it been neglected or misused? If so, you are not ready to offer the sacrifices listed above; your altar cannot receive the fire of God. Isaiah tells us our new name is "Repairer of Broken

Walls" (Isaiah 58:12). We have everything we need in Christ to restore the altar of God in our lives, in our churches and in our ministries. Then we can ask God for His fire to burn on our altars, so that we might fulfill His purpose and build His Kingdom.

QUESTIONS FOR REFLECTION

1. If your personal altar falls into ruin, list the steps you would take and why.

2. Which one of the ten types of ruin is most likely the kind you exhibit when you ignore your relationship with God?

3. How urgent is your desire to keep your family altar fire burning? What will you do this week to nurture that fire?

5

Overthrowing False Altars

Every one of us who truly desires to see the fire and glory of God fall on our altars of worship must be watchmen on the horizons of our lives. If we turn our eyes from worshiping the one true God, we run the risk of His judgment. God spoke clearly to His people about the consequences of their allegiance to false gods:

"Your altars will be demolished and your incense altars will be smashed; and I will slay your people in front of your idols. I will lay the dead bodies of the Israelites in front of their idols, and I will scatter your bones around your altars. Wherever you live, the towns will be laid waste and the high places demolished, so that your altars will be laid waste and devastated, your idols smashed and ruined, your incense altars broken down, and what you have made wiped out."

Ezekiel 6:4–6

As we see throughout much of the Old Testament, all too often the people of God turned from worshiping God to devoting themselves to idols, constructing false altars and bowing before false gods. They neglected the truth and fell into deception. These seasons of idolatry always brought God's judgment on His covenant people.

One example occurred when Manasseh, king of Judah, resurrected altars to Baal, made an Asherah pole and did much evil in the eyes of the Lord. The Lord sent His prophets with the message of judgment:

> "Therefore this is what the LORD, the God of Israel, says: I am going to bring such disaster on Jerusalem and Judah that the ears of everyone who hears of it will tingle. I will stretch out over Jerusalem the measuring line used against Samaria and the plumb line used against the house of Ahab. I will wipe out Jerusalem as one wipes a dish, wiping it and turning it upside down."
>
> 2 Kings 21:12–13

Ultimately, the Lord carried out this judgment by sending them to captivity in Babylon. The price of neglecting the altar and worship of God is very serious. This is a common occurrence in our lives today as well.

Facing the Adversary

The issue for us begins by recognizing that we are engaged in war with a powerful enemy to determine who will receive our worship. Satan, our adversary, has one goal—stop the Lord's people from building an altar to worship Him. The Lord sent Moses with a clear message to Pharaoh: "Let My people go that they may worship Me!" The war with evil is a worship war!

I, Chuck, write about this extensively in *The Future War of the Church*, describing how iniquity builds a false throne or altar on both the personal and corporate levels. Let me say here that Satan's battle plan for overtaking the altar of worship is to lead us into sin. This gives him legal access to our lives:

> Satan continues to exalt himself, attempting to draw all people to his counterfeit light. Satan knows that men and women were created as vessels of worship and, whether they realize it or not, they will worship something. The simple fact is that either they are worshiping the living God or they are worshiping Satan and his demonic forces, whether overtly or through their sin (whether sins of omission or commission). . . .
>
> Sacrifice has great spiritual power. That is why fasting, for example, can be such an effective weapon of warfare. By definition *sacrifice* means "the surrender or destruction of something valued for the sake of something having a higher or more pressing claim." Sin, in our own lives as well as corporately, surrenders the covenant promises of God's blessing for the more pressing claim of whatever the sin promises.
>
> Who ultimately benefits from the sacrifice of sin? Satan and the forces of hell. Just as our sacrificial giving unlocks resources to advance God's covenant plan, sacrifices to Satan release demonic hordes. It is through this sacrifice of sin that Satan sets up a system of worship. In fact, Revelation tells us there is a synagogue of Satan: "I know the blasphemy of those who say they are Jews and are not, but are a synagogue of Satan" (Revelation 2:9 NKJV).*

*Chuck D. Pierce and Rebecca Wagner Sytsema, *The Future War of the Church* (Minneapolis: Chosen, 2014), 111–112.

We must never mix our worship of God with the worship of idols; God will not tolerate divided loyalties. In this chapter we will learn how to clear away the false in preparation for the worship due our Holy God.

The Priesthood Comes Forth

Understanding that we are in a war over worship is key for rekindling the altar fire. Until we destroy any false altar, we cannot move forward in true worship.

We see an example of this war for worship patterned clearly in Scripture from the days of Elijah, extending to Elisha; they were fighting a war over the altar of worship in Israel.

Elijah's well-known question to the people gathered on Mount Carmel was: "How long will you hesitate between two opinions? If the Lord is God, follow Him; but if Baal, follow him." There comes a time when we each must choose what altar we are worshiping from.

The deeper question for the people was this: "Who will rule the worship realm connecting God's people with higher, supernatural power? Will you remain connected with the Holy God who created you as a nation in the earth to demonstrate His power? Or will you realign the nation of Israel with Baal worship and build altars to connect God's people with this demonic empowerment of foreign gods?"

The true God won.

We will look in some detail later at Elijah's power encounter with Queen Jezebel's prophets on Mount Carmel, for this is a classic story—not only in showing the power of God to send fire upon His altar, but also in showing our mandate to overthrow Satan's throne wherever an altar has become established in our lives. The image of the great prophet challenging the confident idol worshipers reveals the magnitude of the war and the place of victory.

But it also shows us something else: We can never become lax in the battle to keep our worship pure. Jezebel was ultimately killed, but there was more to the story. Satan does not give up after a defeat. There was Jezebel's daughter, Athaliah. This evil woman murdered the royal heirs and set herself upon the throne. Her plan was apparently to destroy anything that related to God's covenant promises with His people. For six years she rejected the throne of David and did great evil.

But there came a time when the priesthood rose up to overthrow the evil presence and rebuild the sacred altar. A small child, an heir of the house of David, had been hidden away. He was brought to the Temple, and the priest gave instructions to the military commanders to protect the young king:

> "This is what you shall do: One-third of you who come on duty on the Sabbath shall be keeping watch over the king's house, one-third shall be at the gate of Sur, and one-third at the gate behind the escorts. You shall keep the watch of the house, lest it be broken down. The two contingents of you who go off duty on the Sabbath shall keep the watch of the house of the LORD for the king. But you shall surround the king on all sides, every man with his weapons in his hand; and whoever comes within range, let him be put to death. You are to be with the king as he goes out and as he comes in."
>
> 2 Kings 11:5–8 NKJV

After this, the treacherous queen was seized and killed. Then the people went to the temple of Baal and tore it down, smashing the altars and idols. Under the watchful, faithful eye of the priest, at last, the king could be positioned in his rightful place on the throne. "So all the people of the land rejoiced; and the city was quiet" (2 Kings 11:20 NKJV).

Clearing the Site

We can never let our guard down, for Satan never will. Whenever we detect a false god trying to replace the things of God, it is very important to deal with it before an altar can be built to it. But if we find that there are offerings already being made on a false altar in our hearts, here are four steps for removing that altar and laying a new foundation:

1. Identify the False Altar

The first step in preparing for spiritual renewal and lasting fire on the altar is to identify the false sacrifices we are making.

This only makes sense. It is impossible to experience righteousness until we recognize and deal with sin. We must get rid of the false before we can rebuild the true altar of God and worship Him there. The recognition of false altars is required before a true altar can be restored.

Remember, the altar of the Old Testament is a typology of the cross of Christ. There is no other way or means to be saved but through the death and resurrection of Jesus Christ. All other attempts at salvation are condoning a false altar. When God calls us to repair the altar of true salvation and worship, the process begins with facing up to the places we have made offerings on false altars. Until we are willing to let go of everything false, we are not ready to build or restore the altar of God.

2. Renounce the False God

The next step is also obvious: Having identified the false gods represented by false altars, we must now renounce them.

Suppose, for example, we recognize that we have built a false altar to the god of greed by withholding resources that God has given us for Kingdom work. We renounce it when we open our hands and offer the first portion of what we have to God's purposes and people. We remember the poor with our offerings, and give that which costs us something.

Suppose we recognize that we have built a false altar to the god of lust by polluting our eyes with that which we were never meant to see. The magazine racks and the internet are readily available for the wandering eye—making a mockery of the marriage covenant ordained by God. We identify and renounce that false altar when we refuse to feed illicit thoughts and behavior, and instead give ourselves fully to living in purity within the families God has given us.

Suppose we recognize that we have built a false altar to the god of racism by ignoring unity in Christ and affecting supremacy in our particular culture or heritage. Sunday morning worship is still the most segregated hour of the week in too many places around the world. We renounce those altars when we restore relationships and give ourselves to God to love as He loves.

The list of false altars and the false gods behind them could fill many pages. But our focus is not on them, nor should it be. Identifying and renouncing the altars of false gods demonstrates true zeal for the glory of God.

3. Destroy the False Altar

Once a false altar has been identified, and we have turned our hearts and minds from it, the next step is to demolish it and build a true altar in its place, just as Gideon did.

At the beginning of Gideon's story, when the angel of the Lord appeared to him and gave him the charge to save Israel, Gideon was unsure of himself and asked for a sign. He obtained permission to set out an offering of food.

Gideon followed the instructions he was given regarding the offering, and "the Angel of the LORD put out the end of the staff that was in His hand" and touched the food (Judges 6:21 NKJV). Immediately, "fire flared from the rock, consuming the meat and the bread." Gideon was terrified, surmising that he had encountered the angel of the Lord face-to-face, but the angel said, "Peace! Do not be afraid." So Gideon built an altar and called it "The LORD is Peace" (Judges 6:21–24).

This tells us something very important. Until we have true peace with God, we are not able to destroy the altar of false gods. We need the power, as well as the wisdom, of God. In Gideon's case, once he had established peace with God, the Lord offered him guidance on how to deal with his family's false altar:

> That same night the LORD said to him, "Take the second bull from your father's herd, the one seven years old. Tear down your father's altar to Baal and cut down the Asherah pole beside it. Then build a proper kind of altar to the LORD your God on the top of this height. Using the wood of the Asherah pole that you cut down, offer the second bull as a burnt offering."
>
> Judges 6:25–26

Gideon obeyed God. He destroyed the altar his father had built for a false god and built a far superior altar for God in its place. As a result, Gideon received power from God to complete his mission:

> The Spirit of the LORD came upon Gideon, and he blew a trumpet, summoning the Abiezrites to follow him. He sent messengers throughout Manasseh, calling them to arms, and also into Asher, Zebulun and Naphtali, so that they too went up to meet them.
>
> Judges 6:34–35

As Gideon did, so must we remove false altars and build better altars for our God. As individuals, families and the Body of Christ, we have to deal with false altars—false spirituality, hidden motives, wrong attitudes and whatever we have made first in our lives before the Lord. In doing so, we are cleansing the temples of our bodies just as the Lord Jesus cleansed the Temple in Jerusalem when He turned over the tables of those who were buying and selling in the place of prayer.

4. Remember Your Original Calling

Every altar sits on a foundation. That foundation is the original call to fellowship and worship—the basis of every encounter with God. He puts forth His call, and we respond with our determination and dedication.

This means that for every altar being rebuilt, the only way forward is to go back.

Going back to a solid foundation is crucial for success in dealing with the warfare surrounding altars and removing the false gods we have allowed to stay there. Join us in making

73

these declarations based upon the Word of God so that we are standing once more on a solid foundation and ready to build. Let's move into agreement with His plans for our lives:

- I declare that I love the Lord my God with all my heart and with all my soul and with all my mind;
- I declare, Father in heaven, that Your name is holy. May Your Kingdom come, Your will be done, on earth as it is in heaven;
- I declare that through the blood of Jesus on the cross, I have accepted the hope of salvation. I am reconciled with my heavenly Father and have the promise of eternal life;
- I renounce my former lifestyle when I did not honor the Lord God as first in my life. I renounce all things that are not pleasing to the Lord. I renounce ungodly habits and addictions in my life;
- I declare that my love for my Lord gives me the victory in my life. I am an overcomer and declare that I will serve Him all the days of my life.

Covenant People Choose to Build

God's calling for His covenant people is to worship Him. The starting place for that relationship—and true and lasting victory in His presence—is the altar. We have learned about the vital place of the altar, about how it becomes ruined, about the spiritual warfare against it, and how to dethrone the false altar and recall the foundation for building. In the next chapter, we will discuss how to begin building a true altar of worship in our lives.

QUESTIONS FOR REFLECTION

1. Do you agree that people will worship something—if not God then something else? Why or why not? What false god might you be tempted to put on your altar?

2. What is the status of your altar? Do you remember the time when God called you to build a foundation of worship in your relationship with Him?

3. Do you feel confident about following the steps in this chapter to help you stand firm in the war on worship? Do you feel strong in the things of the Lord? What specific characteristics lead you to your response?

6

Building the Altar of Worship

The altar of worship is the basis for covenant relationship with God and the place where we receive confirmation of our prophetic destinies. That is why Abraham built an altar to the God who revealed Himself to him. In the next generation, Isaac built an altar to confirm that covenant relationship, and, in turn, Jacob set up a pillar and poured oil on it in order to confirm the covenant and receive all that God had promised his grandfather and his father.

The center point of worship and the foundation of covenant relationship with God is the altar. No one who hopes to serve God in any capacity can do so without the altar of worship. Personal renewal must begin with this core issue. Before anything else, we must wholly belong to God.

Let us look at Jacob as an illustration. His parents' village was where he began the search for his prophetic identity, but he was not able to bring it into focus there, much less fulfillment. Instead, he had to leave behind the place where he was raised and go to a place of personal encounter with God. The threat of his brother, Esau, caused him to leave, but he was then able to begin his prophetic journey toward his God-given destiny.

Jacob left Beersheba and set out for Haran, at his parents' direction, both to escape Esau and to seek a wife (see Genesis 28:1–7). When the sun went down, he reached Luz, and he rested for the night. He later changed the name of Luz to *Bethel*, "house of God."

It was not a comfortable place; in fact, Jacob had to use a stone for a pillow. But no other place could have been the starting point for Jacob's prophetic destiny. His grandfather Abraham had built an altar of worship there many years before. It was a place of revelation for Jacob. Heaven was opened. He saw a ladder with angels of God on it. God showed Himself and promised to Jacob the same future as He had promised Abraham and Isaac.

Jacob was awestruck. He took the stone that had been his pillow and made it into an altar of worship, vowing faithfulness to God:

> Then Jacob made a vow, saying, "If God will be with me and will watch over me on this journey I am taking and will give me food to eat and clothes to wear so that I return safely to my father's household, then the LORD will be my God."
>
> Genesis 28:20–21

Scripture gives us no indication that prior to that night Jacob either knew God or worshiped Him. But we do know that it was not until Jacob encountered and responded to the Living God that his prophetic destiny was set into motion. On that one night, in the presence of almighty God, his life changed.

The House of God

Let's look at the events at Bethel and their significance for Jacob's prophetic journey to help us understand what occurs at our personal altars of worship. It is there we begin the process of renewal that is key to relationship with our God. Bethel tells us what it means to have an altar. We will see that Bethel, "house of God," is a place of covenant, revelation, divine appointment, confirmation and God's presence.

Bethel Is a Place of Covenant

Jacob journeyed from his father and mother's house, perhaps not knowing he was initiating his prophetic destiny. At one point in his travels, Jacob chose a spot to spend the night. What made this particular place so important was that Abraham, Jacob's grandfather, had worshiped there years before. In the same place, Abraham had built one of his numerous altars of worship, honoring the One who had earlier revealed Himself with a promise. God had said, "'To your offspring I will give this land.' So he built an altar there to the LORD, who had appeared to him" (Genesis 12:7).

God is a covenant keeper, and that night He renewed with Jacob the promise He had given to Abraham. God spoke to him in a prophetic dream:

> "I am the LORD, the God of your father Abraham and the God of Isaac. I will give you and your descendants the land on which you are lying. Your descendants will be like the dust of the earth, and you will spread out to the west and to the east, to the north and to the south. All peoples on earth will be blessed through you and your offspring. I am with you and will watch over you wherever you go, and I will bring

you back to this land. I will not leave you until I have done what I have promised you."

Genesis 28:13–15

The altar is the place where our covenant relationship with God is established, and He seals us as His own. Years after this experience, after Jacob had faced many trials, the Lord would say to him: "Go up to Bethel and settle there, and build an altar there to God, who appeared to you when you were fleeing from your brother Esau" (Genesis 35:1).

As we read the account of Jacob, we are reminded that the altar we build honors our covenant-keeping God. A true altar of worship gives the promise of victory in our lives—both for us individually and for tomorrow's generations. Another example is found in Joshua 8:12–29, where Joshua conquered the enemy that had defeated them previously at Bethel.

Bethel Is a Place of Revelation

Bethel was the place not only where God revealed Himself, but also where Jacob received revelation about his future. The prophetic dream showed an open heaven with a connecting ladder to earth. The ladder of Jacob's destiny came down without a struggle on his part, and he saw the angels of the Lord ascending and descending on it.

That ladder was the Lord Jesus Christ revealed in the Old Testament. Jesus Himself said, "I tell you the truth, you shall see heaven open, and the angels of God ascending and descending on the Son of Man" (John 1:51). This is a key revelation that we must remember in worship: Prophetic destiny can only be fulfilled through Christ Jesus, who gives us access to the presence of God through His death and resurrection. He is the only way to the revelation and fulfillment of our prophetic destinies.

Bethel Is a Place of Divine Appointment

Jacob received his prophetic destiny before he was born, but he did not hear the Lord's voice until he reached Bethel. That night in his prophetic dream he heard God say, "I am the LORD, the God of your father Abraham and the God of Isaac" (Genesis 28:13).

This revelation was received by divine appointment, at the time and place of God's choosing. This was important for Jacob to hear for several reasons. First, it established his connection to the covenant promises of God. Jacob knew without a shadow of doubt that he was in the plan and purpose of God. Second, it established the authority of God: "I am the Lord." The Lord was saying to Jacob that He was the One who called Abraham and entered into everlasting covenant with him. This divine appointment would establish this covenant with Jacob, as well. Third, it showed that the Lord was in control of Jacob's destiny: "There above [the ladder] stood the LORD, and he said, . . . 'I will give you and your descendants the land on which you are lying'" (Genesis 28:13). In spite of all the struggles Jacob had been through and would go through, the Lord was telling him, *Your prophetic destiny is secured.*

Bethel Is a Place of Confirmation

The Lord looked beyond Jacob's lifetime, telling Jacob that his descendants would possess the land. This is an example of why the altar of worship is crucial to prophetic destiny: This is about future vision. People perish where there is no vision. Without vision there is no hope, and our vision is confirmed at the altar. Part of confirming a prophetic destiny is the release of future covenant blessings. God laid out His covenant blessings to Jacob, and they included multiplication of descendants, divine guidance, protection, fulfillment of the promises and provision (see Genesis 28:14–15).

A prophetic destiny from the Lord comes with full assurance of fulfillment because of the faithfulness of the Promise Giver. Paul affirms this truth: "The one who calls you is faithful and he will do it" (1 Thessalonians 5:24). Paul further assures us: "No matter how many promises God has made, they are 'Yes' in Christ" (2 Corinthians 1:20). This is confirmed at the altar of worship.

Bethel Is a Place of God's Presence

At Bethel, Jacob had an overwhelming experience of God's presence: "When Jacob awoke from his sleep, he thought, 'Surely the LORD is in this place, and I was not aware of it.' He was afraid and said, 'How awesome is this place! This is none other than the house of God; this is the gate of heaven'" (Genesis 28:16–17).

We learn at the altar that the journey of prophetic destiny is not about what we will do at our destinations, but who we will become in the process as we encounter God on the journey. Because Jacob encountered God, the holy fear of God entered into him. He had left his father's house because of the fear of his brother. At Bethel, he experienced the fear of God. The fear of God is the beginning of wisdom, the place at which we discern our prophetic destinies. That desert became the gate of heaven for Jacob. He was overwhelmed by entering the presence of God more than he was by the plans for his future: "How awesome is this place!" That is what building an altar of worship is all about.

The Place of Spiritual Awakening

The awesome presence of God led Jacob into worship. Previously, he had never built an altar of worship. But after encountering God, he took his stone pillow, set it upright, made an altar and poured oil on it. He called the place "house of God," *Bethel*. In doing this, Jacob accepted his prophetic destiny and embraced his future. He made a promise to the Lord to worship and to honor God with his tithing (see Genesis 28:18–22). The Bethel revelation teaches us to set our priorities straight so we can build an altar that honors God. It is the first step toward restoration that leads to lasting personal transformation.

Today, we are called by God to build an altar in our personal lives in order to restore our hearts to our Creator. This is the intimate place of worship where our covenant relationship with God is sealed and where our fellowship is fed and sustained by His life-giving presence. Without building an altar of worship, there can be no further restoration in our lives or true spiritual awakening. Without first building an altar of worship, we cannot function and serve His will on earth as the Lord Jesus did by giving His life to the will of the Father.

Paul explained this. He revealed that our lives not only are to be given in service by *building* an altar but also are to be offered as living sacrifices by *remaining* on the altar, an act of dedication:

> I urge you, brothers, in view of God's mercy, to offer your
> bodies as living sacrifices, holy and pleasing to God—this is

your spiritual act of worship. Do not conform any longer to the pattern of this world, but be transformed by the renewing of your mind. Then you will be able to test and approve what God's will is—his good, pleasing and perfect will.

Romans 12:1–2

This process changes us supernaturally and makes us and our service acceptable to God. Consider these examples from Scripture:

- Purity

    With it he touched my mouth and said, "See, this has touched your lips; your guilt is taken away and your sin atoned for."

    Isaiah 6:7

- Renewal

    "This third I will bring into the fire; I will refine them like silver and test them like gold. They will call on my name and I will answer them; I will say, 'They are my people,' and they will say, 'The LORD is our God.'"

    Zechariah 13:9

- Life

    "I baptize you with water for repentance. But after me will come one who is more powerful than I. . . . He will baptize you with the Holy Spirit and with fire."

    Matthew 3:11

- Empowerment

    Suddenly a sound like the blowing of a violent wind came from heaven and filled the whole

house where they were sitting. They saw what
seemed to be tongues of fire that separated and
came to rest on each of them.

Acts 2:2–3

- Passion for God
  "Every morning the priest is to add firewood
  and arrange the burnt offering on the fire. . . . The
  fire must be kept burning on the altar continuously; it must not go out."

Leviticus 6:12–13

God's command was to construct an altar on which sacrifices and offerings would be placed. His resulting promise
was to come and bless, not the altar, but the person who
built it.

Lasting Fire

It is crucial that we become altar builders whose very lives
invite the fire of God, because every believer in every generation seeks the blessing—and the blessing is connected to the
fire. Without the fire and presence of God, we will quietly and
desperately lead the lives of servants, not children; of hired
hands, not heirs to a Kingdom. When Esau lost his father's
blessing, his desperation was heart-wrenchingly painful.

It is not our responsibility to provide the fire; that is God's
part. But we must prepare a place for the fire of God by building the altar of worship. That is why the primary activity of
our day must be maintenance of the altar in our lives. There
cannot be a lasting fire without an enduring altar!

We will look more closely at the altars of worship in both
the Tabernacle and the Temple, but note here that on the

days of dedication, once God found the sacrifice acceptable and sent His fire from heaven, it became the responsibility of the priests to keep the fire burning. It was not a simple matter. It required attentiveness, diligence and commitment to the things of God. If the fire went out, the sacrifice would not be consumed, and the priests were not permitted to start the fire again. The fire of God could not be duplicated by mere men, even priests.

Today, when we build the altar of a pure, wholehearted relationship with our God, and when He approves of our sacrifice and sends His holy fire down from heaven—our responsibility is to keep His fire burning. As in Old Testament times, this requires attentiveness, diligence and commitment to the things of God; an unwavering, undivided love for His beloved Son and the cross where His Son redeemed humankind. That love must be kept alive through our relationship with Him with ever-increasing love and worship.

In Revelation 2:1–7 we read that the Holy Spirit spoke to the church in Ephesus and praised them for their perseverance for His name's sake. He had one thing against them, however: They had left their first love. The love relationship was gone. God commands us to "love the LORD your God with all your heart and with all your soul and with all your strength" (Deuteronomy 6:5).

You build an altar by making sure your priorities are straight. By honoring God in your heart. By embracing the future He has for you. By keeping your love relationship with Him strong. When you build, He sends the fire.

Then, once God sends the fire, you are ready to explore new places in this relationship. In the chapters that follow, we will learn crucial lessons for building and caring for an altar, maintaining it even while abiding in wilderness places.

QUESTIONS FOR REFLECTION

1. How does this teaching about Bethel help you set your priorities? Where might you have fallen short in constructing an altar of worship?

2. Have you let God's fire go out on the altar of your life? If so, how might this be affecting the revelation of your prophetic destiny?

3. Will you commit to be a keeper of the flame?

7

Making Your Altar a Priority

Anytime we recognize that our altars need to be rebuilt—or perhaps built for the first time—and we set out to make right the place of worship, our urgency pleases God. John Dickson, one of our senior worship leaders at Glory of Zion International, shared this personal story with us, and we want to share it with you:

> The altar is always where you return! The reasons you left might be many and varied. You got busy with other things. Life took you in another direction. You found something else to take its place. But when crisis comes in your life, you remember, "Ah, the altar. That's where I met God. That's where I found my true person and calling." And from this realization, you return and rebuild the fallen stones—the stones of your original commitment, the stones of your vows to God, the stones that remind you of His visitation. The patriarchs built their altars after visitations or to mark their commitments. At times, God led them back to those altars

to remember or recommit. The altars remained even after their deaths for others to come to and reconnect with God.

We all have altars in our lives as well, times when the Lord has visited us or when we made a commitment. These might be things we have forgotten in our busy lives. They might be promises we need to revisit. Our altars can be like an anchor of a ship that is being blown in a storm.

Almost forty years ago, the Lord told my wife, Violet, and me to move to Denton, Texas, because we had grown as much as we could where we were. I was longing for an apostle to father me, though we did not use that term back then. It was a leap of faith from a place where we had a home, a business and a ministry to a place where I did not even have a job. Over the next two years things got very disheartening, but we were faithful to look to the commitment we had made on that altar when we left everything behind. It was an anchor for us in very turbulent waters. We hung on to it, believing that we had heard God.

We ended up on the back row of a small church where I was eventually invited to become the worship leader.

A couple of years later Chuck Pierce joined that church. He was the apostle my heart had been searching for when we made the move to Denton. Under his hand my giftings began to quicken, and the church eventually became Glory of Zion. My whole future was able to open up because we never forgot the altar. The winds blew and the storms raged, but the anchor held.

There is a story of the old Chinese saint Watchman Nee. He was walking along a beach with a cane because of an injured knee when the Lord visited him, and his knee was healed. He rammed the cane into the sand and left it because he longer needed it.

A while later his knee began to pain him again. He walked back to where he had put the cane in the sand and shouted,

"This is where the Lord healed my knee." It was for him the place of remembrance of the Lord's visitation—the place of his declaration—His altar.

We can erect an altar where God visits us and say, "This is what I stand by." When things get difficult, we look back at that altar and say, "I'm sticking with this."

And after we come through hard times, we remember His faithfulness there as well. Samuel did this. As the Philistines were coming to attack Israel, Samuel was praying to the Lord, crying out on Israel's behalf:

> While Samuel was sacrificing the burnt offering, the Philistines drew near to engage Israel in battle. But that day the LORD thundered with loud thunder against the Philistines and threw them into such a panic that they were routed before the Israelites. The men of Israel rushed out of Mizpah and pursued the Philistines. . . . Then Samuel took a stone and set it up between Mizpah and Shen. He named it Ebenezer, saying, "Thus far has the LORD helped us." So the Philistines were subdued and did not invade Israelite territory again.
>
> 1 Samuel 7:10–13

Sometimes God comes and builds an altar of His own in us. Ten years ago, I was at what I thought to be a good place in my gifts, my calling and my ministry. God came to me in a worship service and put me on the floor during the ministry time. He gave me a chapter in Isaiah as a covenant with me and then began a process of disassembling my gifts, my calling and my ministry.

It was, thankfully, not evident to anyone but me, but it was a devastating season. He told me He was going to build something new in me, and it was necessary to tear down in order for Him to plant. I complained that He was tearing down all the good stuff and that I had plenty of bad stuff that I would love for Him to tear down, but I bore it because of the altar He had built: the chapter in Isaiah. As time went on, His pruning cut me down to the quick, yet there was no sign of the new growth He had promised. All along, though, I clung to that altar of His making. It went on for years. I felt like Sarah, getting older every year and way past the age for conception.

Finally, almost ten years later, Chuck spoke a word to me, and something in me began to quicken. Then little by little something new began to grow in me. Eventually it began to bloom, and I began to understand what the previous ten years had been all about.

When God visited me, I had been the sole worship leader at Glory of Zion for the previous 25 years. Others were alongside me, but no one felt confident to step into that lead position, though I had encouraged them to do so. When God laid me down to build His altar in me, He began to bring others out into their leadership callings. Over the next few years, a broad front of leaders emerged, all with their own unique ministry styles, and God began to move me into my new place behind them. I loved it. I would have never thought of it.

Then God spoke to me, *Eye has not seen, nor ear heard, nor has entered into your heart the things I have for you.* We just have to cling to the altar He has built in us.

An altar cannot be blown down by the wind; it can only be torn down by our own hands. If we forget the altars, if we tire of them, if we move on from them, the stones slowly crumble. But if we return, if we remember, if we stand firm, the stones remain.

I have a mezuzah on my doorpost at home. This is a small hollow ornament such as Jews put Scriptures in and affix to their doorposts, as God commanded in Deuteronomy

6:9 (NKJV): "You shall write them on the doorposts of your house." *Mezuzah* actually means "doorpost." Mine has the Scriptures and the promises that God has given to me. It is my "mini altar" to remind me every time I walk through my front door.

Without the altar of God signifying the cross, there is no life, no hope and no spiritual blessing. All of our spiritual needs can be met only through the work of the cross. That is why the Word of God calls us to "approach the throne of grace with confidence, so that we may receive mercy and find grace to help us in our time of need" (Hebrews 4:16).

The altar is common ground in our relationships with our God. At the altar, the cross of Christ, we are cleansed from our sins and receive a clean conscience to worship and obey His will. The altar is where we understand the depth of His love, His eternal purposes and His destiny for our lives. The altar is where we receive daily victory. That is the reason Paul said, "I want to know Christ and the power of his resurrection and the fellowship of sharing in his sufferings, becoming like him in his death" (Philippians 3:10).

We can say that we are more than conquerors through him who loved us (see Romans 8:37) only when we have a true relationship with our Redeemer at the altar. This builds confidence in us to accept His call and respond that "I can do everything through him who gives me strength" (Philippians 4:13). The source of such spiritual confidence is not the pride that comes from depending on our own strength; it is the wisdom that comes from knowing what was already accomplished for us at the altar. Jesus summed it up bravely on the cross: "It is finished."

An Exchange Takes Place

For a child of God, the altar is not only a place of receiving, but also a place of giving. There we give our lives back to God: "You were bought at a price. Therefore honor God with your body" (1 Corinthians 6:20).

If, then, we believe that the altar is a place of giving to God what He deserves as well as receiving all the blessings He has for us, then restoring the altar of God becomes a very urgent endeavor. Restoring the altar enables us to worship the Lord in spirit and in truth. This is the desire of God the Father as Jesus Himself described it: "Yet a time is coming and has now come when the true worshipers will worship the Father in spirit and truth, for they are the kind of worshipers the Father seeks" (John 4:23). Restoring the altar is about spiritual renewal, restoration and revival to offer God what He desires: "God is spirit, and his worshipers must worship in spirit and in truth" (verse 24).

The building or restoration of an altar is a new season, a new beginning. And the foundation of any new beginning is establishing our relationship with God through sincere and true worship. A new season in our lives means hearing, understanding and obeying the voice of God, wholeheartedly. That puts us on a new path.

Without a proper altar, we cannot offer a proper sacrifice, and we cannot receive what God has for us. We would not be able to bring our bodies as living sacrifices, including our spiritual gifts, talents, abilities and resources, to glorify Him. Without an altar, there is no place for sacrifice. Without a place for sacrifice, there is no holy fire of God. Without a holy fire of God, there is no manifest glory of God or spiritual revival. The end result is lifeless, dead religion; clouds without rain.

Dead religion kills rather than saves, sickens rather than heals and condemns rather than frees. It is not dead religion but the love of Christ that says to sinners: "Neither do I condemn you. . . . Go now and leave your life of sin" (John 8:11).

That is why an altar for a fire of God's love, mercy, grace, life, joy and peace must be top priority. When we restore the altar, we focus not on what we can do for God, but on what God has done for us. When the Israelites neglected the altar, they did not remember what God had done for them. Whenever they truly repented of neglecting or destroying the altar of God, their next step was to restore it. As we will discuss in the next chapter, this is exactly what the prophet Elijah did before he asked God to come and consume a very wet sacrifice on Mount Carmel.

The Priority of Fire for Ministry

John the Baptist knew that a servant of God is one who has been touched by the fire of God. As John would baptize with water, the coming Messiah would baptize with water and fire. Water baptism signifies the death of the old life in the flesh and separation to a new spiritual life in Christ Jesus: The fire of God follows salvation. Jesus Christ gives not only life, but also the fire of the Holy Spirit to make us capable for ministry.

Having prepared His disciples, Jesus gave them this order: "I am going to send you what my Father has promised; but stay in the city until you have been clothed with power from on high" (Luke 24:49).

Their ministry could not begin until the fire fell. The obedient disciples remained in Jerusalem. They waited in worship and prayer until they were baptized with fire on the Day of Pentecost (see Acts 2:1–4). God uses us as instruments of His glory only after purifying us with His fire, awakening our spirits, renewing our lives, breaking the chains of sin and burning down our egos.

The fire of the Holy Spirit cleanses, sanctifies, beautifies and changes a person into the likeness of Jesus Christ. God uses this process to make "His ministers a flame of fire" (Psalm 104:4 NKJV). This verse speaks of His angels, His messengers (see Hebrews 1:7), but the fire of God also renews God's people to declare His glory with full authority as His "sent ones" or messengers.

When Isaiah, a prophet, saw the Lord in His greatness and majesty, he cried out because of his own personal unworthiness:

> Then one of the seraphs flew to me with a live coal in his hand, which he had taken with tongs from the altar. With it he touched my mouth and said, "See, this has touched your lips; your guilt is taken away and your sin atoned for."
>
> Then I heard the voice of the LORD saying, "Whom shall I send? And who will go for us?"
>
> And I said, "Here am I. Send me!"
>
> Isaiah 6:6–8

The fire of consecration touched him by removing the guilt, enabled him to hear the call of God and empowered him to respond without delay.

The Priority of Holiness in Fire

The fire of God brings holiness into the lives of His servants for true relationship to enhance the kind of worship that

Diagram of the Tabernacle

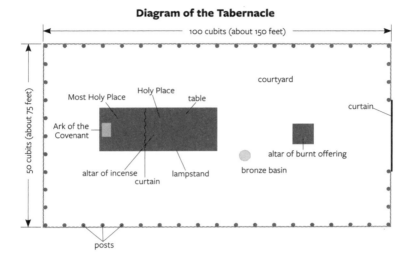

pleases Him. It cleanses the tongue, making servants deserving speakers of the Lord. It cleanses our image, so we can reflect the life of the Lord.

Let us look at an example that illustrates this.

When the fire of God comes to us, we are conformed to the likeness of His Son. In true worship the fire enables us to meet God with a personal encounter. Remember that the altar is where the fire of God is burning continuously. Without the altar we cannot keep His fire burning. Without the fire there cannot be true worship.

As you can see from the diagram above, worship begins at the altar of burnt offering and goes all the way to the altar of incense before we enter into His presence through the work of the cross of Christ.

It is described beautifully in the book of Hebrews:

Therefore, brothers, since we have confidence to enter the Most Holy Place by the blood of Jesus, by a new and living way opened for us through the curtain, that is, his body, and since we have a great priest over the house of God, let us draw near to God with a sincere heart in full assurance of faith, having our hearts sprinkled to cleanse us from a guilty conscience and having our bodies washed with pure water.

Hebrews 10:19–22

This makes clear that we start worship at the altar and go all the way through to the throne room of the King of glory, our Savior and Redeemer who qualified us by His own blood: "To him who loves us and has freed us from our sins by his blood, and has made us to be a kingdom and priests to serve his God and Father—to him be glory and power for ever and ever! Amen" (Revelation 1:5–6). That is why the Lord measures both the altar and the worshipers: "Then I [the apostle John] was given a reed like a measuring rod. And the angel stood, saying, 'Rise and measure the temple of God, the altar, and those who worship there'" (Revelation 11:1 NKJV).

The Fire for Daily Victory

The basis of our salvation is what the Lord Jesus, the Lamb of God, did for us on the cross. John the Baptist declared this truth when he introduced the Lord Jesus by saying, "Look, the Lamb of God, who takes away the sin of the world!" (John 1:29).

An altar is a place of divine encounter through the cross of Christ. It is a point of contact to receive mercy and grace for salvation, the power of the Holy Spirit for sonship and worship. We are able to enter into His holy presence for everlasting covenant and ongoing renewal of life to reflect His glory as we are being transformed into His image.

98

An altar is a place of moment-by-moment surrender of one's will. Only by making this surrender a priority can we dwell together in harmony with God. "I no longer live, but Christ lives in me" (Galatians 2:20). "I die daily" (1 Corinthians 15:31 NKJV). "Offer your bodies as a living sacrifice" (Romans 12:1). It is no longer our will or personal interests that matter; everything we have and are belongs to Jesus.

Do you sense the urgency? Until we come to the altar, the place of sacrifice, and give Him our lives in total commitment, Jesus Christ has not become our Lord and King (see Romans 14:7). As Jesus said obediently, so we say, "Father . . . not my will but yours be done" (Luke 22:42). Staying at the altar, for a believer, is dwelling in holy covenant communion with the Living God; a lifestyle of obedience. This is what it means to be living sacrifices for a Living God.

At the altar, the cross of Christ, we are cleansed from our sins and are given a clean conscience to worship and obey His will. The altar is where we understand the depth of His love, His eternal purpose and His destiny for our lives. That altar is where we receive daily victory. That is the reason Paul said, "I want to know Christ and the power of his resurrection and the fellowship of sharing in his sufferings, becoming like him in his death" (Philippians 3:10).

Until we make this commitment at the altar, we cannot understand that "we are more than conquerors through him who loved us" (Romans 8:37). But when we come with heartfelt urgency, we gain confidence to accept His call by responding, "I can do everything through him who gives me strength" (Philippians 4:13). The source of such spiritual confidence is not pride in our own strength, but receiving gratefully what was already accomplished for us at the altar.

As Jesus gave His life on the cross for us, we are called to give our lives as living sacrifices to live for His glory daily, without hesitation or delay: "Therefore, I urge you, brothers, in view of God's mercy, to offer your bodies as living sacrifices, holy and pleasing to God—this is your spiritual act of worship" (Romans 12:1). There we give our lives back to God: "You were bought at a price. Therefore honor God with your body" (1 Corinthians 6:20). The giving of our lives at the altar includes our praise, obedience in doing His will, ministry to others and living for Him by doing everything for His glory, all the time.

This is our goal—this is the foundation of a new beginning in our relationship with God. Otherwise, if we grow slack in the care of the altar of God, we ignore not only the abundant life He has for us, but also our responsibilities in responding to His eternal love.

The Israelites learned this lesson the hard way. It took two of the greatest leaders in her long history to teach God's people what it means to keep the fire burning, and the devastation that comes from letting it go. Let's look at them now, so we can make fresh our desire for God's altar to be the priority of our lives every single day.

QUESTIONS FOR REFLECTION

1. Why is an altar the foundation for our salvation and blessings?
2. Why is it so urgent to restore the altar, and how do you go about it?
3. As you think about the diagram of the Tabernacle and your own life, how close are you to the Most Holy Place—meaning, keeping your altar in good repair? Are you encouraged by your progress? Why or why not?

8

Keeping the Altar Fire Burning

A new beginning, new season or journey of destiny requires either building a new altar or restoring an altar once it has fallen into disrepair. God will meet us at both places, but only if our hearts are sincere. Let's look in more depth at the lessons God taught His people through Moses about keeping the fire burning, and Elijah's battle for restoration when God's people let the fire go out.

Moses: The Place of the Altar

When God wanted to set His people free from slavery in Egypt, He revealed Himself to Moses from a burning bush. Moses went to investigate the fire, and he heard God's voice. In obedience he left Midian and carried God's message to Pharaoh: "Let My people go so that they may worship Me."

Before leaving their bondage in Egypt, the Israelites followed the instructions for marking their doorposts with the blood of lambs, the event they would remember and celebrate every year as Passover. The Lord had told them, "When I see the blood on your doorposts, I will pass over you. The destroyer of the firstborn will not enter your house" (see Exodus 12:13; Hebrews 11:28). They recognized the redemption of God.

After passing safely through the Red Sea, Israel again witnessed the Lord's protection from the enemy. This time they took another step toward true worship by picking up instruments and singing songs of victory to the Lord, praising Him for what He had done and reflecting on His goodness. At that point, the Lord instructed Moses to have the people "make a sanctuary for me, and I will dwell among them" (Exodus 25:8). The Tabernacle with its altar fire was so crucial to their understanding of relationship that the Lord halted their journey and gave instructions for building Him a place of worship.

Some undoubtedly wanted to press on toward their destination, thinking, "Lord, can't You wait until we enter the Promised Land?" No! True adoration and worship is not for tomorrow; it is for the present! The Lord wanted Israel to understand and confirm His covenant with them at the very beginning of their journey. Sometimes in our Christian walks, we want to wait until we have victory, or see God's purpose or promises fulfilled, before we worship the Lord and give Him heartfelt adoration and praise. This should not be so. We should start praising God right where we are.

Notice that the instructions for worshiping God had their basis in the Law given to Moses. There are three points to keep in mind—specific instructions that apply to us as we study the care of the altar:

- First, the Lord wanted His people *to know Him*. He gave the Law to show how holy and awesome He is and help them understand His character;
- Second, the Lord wanted His people *to honor Him*. He showed them, through the Law, how to approach Him through the ceremonies of the Tabernacle;
- Third, the Lord wanted His people *to be in fellowship with Him*. The Law brought them into fellowship with God through offerings—sin offerings, guilt offerings, fellowship offerings, grain offerings and burnt offerings.

As we have noted, a burnt offering meant that something was entirely consumed by fire as a sign of God's acceptance. The Hebrew word for *burnt* ('ôlâh) means "that which goes up to God." The offering was consumed completely, an act that signified total dedication. It was given to the Lord as an act of worship, an acknowledgment that the sacrifice belonged to Him. This was complete consecration; an expression of surrender to God.

With this background in view, let's look at God's directions to Moses for care of the altar.

Instructions for Altar Care

In Leviticus 6, we read specific instructions that the Lord gave the Israelites regarding the altar and the offerings presented on it. These Old Testament instructions also form a typology or example that we can relate to as followers of Christ.

From the following nine instructions, we can apply to our lives the spiritual implications for New Testament worship, and especially prayer:

1. The Burnt Offering Must Remain on the Altar

"The burnt offering is to remain on the altar hearth throughout the night, till morning" (Leviticus 6:9). What belongs to the Lord may not be taken off the altar, put somewhere else and returned later. It must stay on the altar until the fire from the Lord consumes and consecrates it. Our burnt offerings—our praise, worship, adoration and prayer—should always remain before the Lord. What we bring to Him cannot be handled however we please, however we choose. If you dedicate your life to the Lord, it must stay dedicated. If you devote your talent, it must remain devoted. What you offer to the Lord must be kept on His altar.

2. Only the Lord's Fire May Be Used for Worship

"Fire came out from the presence of the Lord and consumed the burnt offering and the fat portions on the altar. And when all the people saw it, they shouted for joy" (Leviticus 9:24). The fire that consumed the burnt offerings came from God; it was not man-made.

Sometimes in our Christian walks, instead of going to God and asking Him to send His fire, we start our own fires. We then try to fan that fleshly fire through activities, events or programs. But human fire is very destructive. For every human fire we start in the house of the Lord, particularly in spiritual ministry, a price must be paid directly or indirectly either today or in the future.

We see an example of this after the priests began their ministry at the Tabernacle when the two oldest sons of Aaron, the high priest, disobeyed God. No sooner had the fire from the Lord come and consumed the burnt offering on the altar, than Nadab and Abihu "offered unauthorized fire before the LORD, contrary to his command" (Leviticus 10:1; see Leviticus 9:24).

Aaron's sons, planning to offer incense within the Tabernacle, went ahead and started their own fire rather than taking from God's fire that was burning on the altar. We read that they were punished by death for this sacrilege of bringing counterfeit fire before the Lord: "Fire came out from the presence of the LORD and consumed them, and they died" (Leviticus 10:2). The old adage about playing with fire is true: You will eventually get burned.

Because of God's grace and mercy through Christ Jesus, He no longer does such things under the New Covenant. We need to remember, however, that God's grace does not change His attributes. God was holy in the Old Testament, and He is holy today. God was a consuming fire in the Old Testament, and He is a consuming fire today.

What is the difference between the Old Testament and current times? Today God's grace allows us to approach Him at His throne. But never forget: His attributes have not changed. Our God is unchanging. He is the same yesterday, today and forevermore.

Thus, we must never create things of the flesh and call them things of God. We must never mix the divine with the human. False fire is what we create when the presence of God is not real in our lives. We avoid false fire by being sincere, honest and true with God, by understanding, obeying and submitting fully to His will.

3. The Altar Fire Must Be Kept Burning

"The fire must be kept burning on the altar" (Leviticus 6:9). The important thing to keep in mind here is that the worshipers did not start the fire; but once God had ignited it, the people were responsible to keep it burning day and night. God wanted this so they would not create their own fires for their sacrifices and offerings. When each burnt offering was appropriately prepared, it was put on the altar. The fire consumed it to signify that He accepted the offering.

4. The Ashes Must Be Removed

"The priest . . . shall remove the ashes of the burnt offering that the fire has consumed on the altar" (Leviticus 6:10). The Lord told the priests to remove the ashes because leftover ashes contribute nothing to a fresh fire. Indeed, a fresh fire can be smothered by the remains of a previous fire. They needed to clean out the ashes of God's fire to maintain the purity of the altar.

Purity is essential in worship, praise, adoration and prayer. After performing His first miracle, Jesus went to the Temple and overturned the tables where animals for sacrifices and money were changing hands. He said, "Get these out of here! How dare you turn my Father's house into a market!" (John 2:16). People were using the house of God for personal gain. We might see evidence of this very condition in our own lives in the way we make and use money. This is very important for worship. In fact, we cannot separate from worship the way we use money. In most cases, the way we relate to and handle money reflects the way we worship God.

We must keep the altar pure and clean, being particularly careful not to be motivated by personal gain. Those who are pure in heart will see the Lord in their worship. Purity is a sign of holiness. Holiness is not legalism, but rather a desire to be more like Him, to be changed into His likeness.

5. *The Ashes Must Be Taken outside the Camp*

"Then he is to . . . carry the ashes outside the camp to a place that is ceremonially clean" (Leviticus 6:11). Not only must ashes be cleaned from the altar, but they must be completely removed.

What does this mean for us? Paul said, "You were taught . . . to put off your old self" (Ephesians 4:22), and added, "Do not let any unwholesome talk come out of your mouths, but only what is helpful for building others up according to their needs. . . . Do not grieve the Holy Spirit of God, with whom you were sealed for the day of redemption" (Ephesians 4:29–30). Then he explained what needed to be removed from the Israelite camp; and ours, too: "All bitterness, rage and anger, brawling and slander, along with every form of malice" (Ephesians 4:31).

These are the ashes we need to remove from our altars so we do not grieve the Holy Spirit or put out His fire.

6. *Firewood Must Be Added Every Morning*

"Every morning the priest is to add firewood" (Leviticus 6:12). The Lord told the priests to add firewood early each day. This kept the fire burning with a vigorous flame.

Those things that help us grow in relationship with the Lord and keep our spiritual fires burning are crucial to our spiritual well-being: reading the Word, Christian fellowship, prayer, accountability, sitting under anointed teaching and submitting ourselves to the right kind of authority.

7. The Burnt Offerings Must Be Arranged

"Every morning the priest is to . . . arrange the burnt offering on the fire" (Leviticus 6:12). The priests were instructed to arrange the burnt offerings, but they were not instructed to create the fire. This is an illustration of the importance of divine order. Where there is no divine order, or where divine order is not observed, true and sincere worship according to the Word of God cannot take place. Further, where divine order is lacking, there is no effective prayer. Obedience to divine order is vital, especially where the moving of the Holy Spirit is evident.

This is crucial for the next move of God in today's society. Things must be done not according to human logic, desires, philosophy, religious practices or experience, but according to divine order based upon the Word of God. The issue is not what we feel, but rather what God's Word says. It is not what we have experienced that is important, but rather the truth in God's Word.

We see divine order laid out clearly in the protocol that the Holy Spirit provided the Church. He has given us the fivefold ministries of the Holy Spirit, the gifts of the Holy Spirit and the fruit of the Holy Spirit. Note that the fivefold ministries named in Ephesians 4:11—apostles, prophets, evangelists, pastors and teachers—are given to unite people who have the *gifts* of the Holy Spirit, so they can bear the *fruit* of the Spirit. Divine order is established in the Church where the fivefold ministries operate. God gives spiritual authority in churches so ministry can flow according to His purpose.

8. *The Fat of the Offerings Must Be Burned*

"Every morning the priest is to . . . burn the fat of the fellowship offerings" (Leviticus 6:12). In the Old Testament, fat refers to the best part of the sacrifice. God desires our best and must be offered the best. In worship, and especially in our prayer lives, if we bring leftovers, such as our tired and exhausted hours, God is not honored, and we are not effective. If we are sincere about prayer and worship, we need to give God our best. The instruction in the Old Testament was to bring God the best, because God is worthy of our best.

9. *The Altar Must Never Be Defiled*

"If any of you . . . presents a gift for a burnt offering to the LORD . . . you must present a male without defect from the cattle, sheep or goats in order that it may be accepted on your behalf. Do not bring anything with a defect" (Leviticus 22:18–20). This shows further damaging effects of not bringing our best: A blemished animal actually defiled the altar. Under the New Covenant, we defile the altar if we come to Him purposely not seeking His will or listening to what He is saying. Indeed, every time we bring worship that comes from impure hearts and wrong motives, we defile His altar.

Anytime we ignore the purposes of God, bringing Him our leftovers and saving our best for pursuits other than worship, we defile the altar.

Never Neglect a Burning Fire

We see from these verses that it is a crucial point of altar care that the fire be maintained in proper order. Sin and rebellion extinguish the fire of God, and when that happens, everything is gone. Read again these verses in which the Lord warned the Israelites not to allow the Tabernacle altar fire to go out:

> The LORD said to Moses: "Give Aaron and his sons this command. . . . The burnt offering is to remain on the altar hearth throughout the night, till morning, and the fire must be kept burning on the altar. . . . The fire on the altar must be kept burning; it must not go out. Every morning the priest is to add firewood and arrange the burnt offering on the fire and burn the fat of the fellowship offerings on it. The fire must be kept burning on the altar continuously; it must not go out."
>
> Leviticus 6:8–9, 12–13

In this short passage, the Lord told them three times not to let the fire go out. Every time the fire was neglected, the presence of God—His provision, protection and guidance—was removed. We see this reality—neglect of the fire on the altar, ruin of the altar and the subsequent removal of God's presence—all through the Old Testament. Whenever the Israelites let the altar go to ruin, there was no fire of God; no presence of God. Which brings us to Elijah.

Elijah: When the Fire Goes Out

About six centuries had passed from the time the Israelites had received the instructions from Moses about diligence

112

toward the altar, and in far too many instances, they had not heeded his words. Solomon's kingdom had been torn in two by strife, and the Northern tribes of Israel, under King Ahab, no longer worshiped at the Temple in Jerusalem, which was held by the Southern tribes of Judah.

This time of Elijah's ministry with Ahab as king was a desperate time. The land was gripped by the drought he had prophesied. Prophets were hiding in caves, as Queen Jezebel plotted their demise, and the tangible power and promises of God were a distant memory. The Gentiles who inhabited the land surrounding Israel were immersed in idol worship. "The altar of the Lord" (1 Kings 18:30) located at Carmel, undoubtedly an old and sacred place of worship because of the respect Elijah gave it, had been neglected.

Quite clearly, the fire in Israel had gone out.

The Israelites, who always longed to be like the Gentiles, rebelled against God in five specific ways:

1. They Rebelled against God's Laws

During this time of widespread idol worship, the entire nation of Israel had left the Lord and shifted their hearts to other gods: "The angel of the LORD said to Elijah the Tishbite, 'Go up and meet the messengers of the king of Samaria and ask them, "Is it because there is no God in Israel that you are going off to consult Baal-Zebub, the god of Ekron?"' . . . So Elijah went" (2 Kings 1:3–4).

2. They Abandoned Their Service to God

Because they were not serving God, the altar of God was neglected and fell into ruin.

3. *Their Kings Refused to Serve the Lord*

Since they disliked listening to God's prophets, the kings hired their own prophets who spoke falsehoods. These false prophets hindered the people from coming to truth and returning to the Lord through repentance.

4. *Ahab and Jezebel Persecuted God's Prophets*

Wicked Queen Jezebel persecuted God's prophets mercilessly. A servant of King Ahab witnessed this to Elijah: "Haven't you heard, my lord, what I did while Jezebel was killing the prophets of the LORD? I hid a hundred of the LORD's prophets in two caves, fifty in each, and supplied them with food and water" (1 Kings 18:13). Her persecutions were intense enough to drive God's prophets into hiding.

The Scriptures reveal that this was a time of active persecution by the king as well. The servant said further to Elijah: "There is not a nation or kingdom where my master has not sent someone to look for you. And whenever a nation or a kingdom claimed you were not there, he made them swear they could not find you" (1 Kings 18:10). You can sense the discomfort others felt by even being around the prophets of God: "Now you tell me to go to my master and say, 'Elijah is here.' He will kill me!" (1 Kings 18:14). This demonstrates how men of this period failed to hear God's voice. Little wonder that Jezebel wanted to kill Elijah.

5. *Ahab and Jezebel Persecuted the Priests*

The priests who were left were forced to disperse. Consequently, there was no one to stand before the Lord and offer sacrifices. The altar was abandoned, and spiritual ministry ceased. Idolatrous priests who offered sacrifices to false gods replaced the priests of God.

Unfortunately, these points are also descriptive of large parts of the Body of Christ. Lacking fresh fire from God, many Christians do their best to live without it, and then wonder why their enemy seems so strong, why they have no power to overcome sin, why they cannot live what they confess, and the list could go on.

After many years of secret prayer and waiting (such as you may have experienced), the prophet Elijah was finally directed by God to emerge from hiding and reveal himself to King Ahab. It appears that the Lord is saying today that it is time for His people to do the same. He is calling His Church to emerge from our caves and rebuild the altars of our lives, families, churches, cities and nations so He can release His fire upon them.

In obedience to the word of the Lord, and despite great personal risk, Elijah confronted Ahab. The king agreed to assemble the people of Israel and the prophets of Baal on Mount Carmel, and when they had all gathered, Elijah issued his challenge. He said in essence, "Who would intentionally worship a false god? Who would intentionally live without fire and rain? Let us cry out—the prophets of Baal at their altar and the people of God at His altar—and let us follow the God who answers by fire and the God who sends the rain!"

In accordance with the agreement, the prophets of Baal prepared an offering and called on their god. But there was no answer, either by fire or sound. After a fruitless day of pleading, shouting and cutting themselves, the prophets of Baal surrendered and consented that their god had no fire.

Elijah knew that for straying, rebellious hearts to return fully to God, they needed to experience His fire, and for such a fire to burn, the true altar must be restored.

The Process of Rekindling

We learn from Elijah that certain preparations preceded God's glorifying of His name by fire. Elijah's preparations included the following five areas:

1. Elijah Saw the Need for Repair

"Elijah said to all the people, 'Come here to me.' They came to him, and he repaired the altar of the LORD, which was in ruins" (1 Kings 18:30). For God's fire to fall, the altar had to be made ready and built on a sure foundation. The life of praise, worship and prayer experienced at the altar should be renewed by the study of the Word. Isaiah makes this clear in his teaching on fasting (see Isaiah 58).

2. Elijah Recalled Israel's Heritage

"Elijah took twelve stones, one for each of the tribes descended from Jacob, to whom the word of the LORD had come, saying, 'Your name shall be Israel.' With the stones he built an altar in the name of the LORD" (1 Kings 18:31). Elijah built the altar with twelve stones to remind the people of their heritage as God's chosen nation.

This was an important point of identification for them, and it would help highlight their need for repentance. At times it is necessary to intercede for the people of God by repenting on their behalf. The Lord respects this. We see

116

Daniel doing this (see Daniel 9). Nehemiah also fasted and confessed the sins of his people (see Nehemiah 1).

3. Elijah Followed the Lord's Timetable

"At the time of sacrifice, the prophet Elijah stepped forward and prayed" (1 Kings 18:36). A servant who wants the fire of God must forego his calendar and be willing to do everything according to God's timing, not rushing ahead or lagging behind. God has His own calendar. Since He is Lord of time, His timing is always perfect.

4. Elijah Acted According to God's Word

Elijah prayed, "O LORD, God of Abraham, Isaac and Israel, let it be known today that you are God in Israel and that I am your servant and have done all these things at your command" (1 Kings 18:36). God is Lord, faithful to His words and, therefore, unfailing in everything He promises.

5. Elijah Prayed a Prayer of Faith

Elijah's faith at this point is more than astonishing. The altar had been repaired. The wood and the sacrifice had been placed upon it, and it had all been doused with water to the extent that water filled the trench encircling it. Hundreds of false prophets, bleeding from their frenzy, were looking on, certain that he would fail as they had. The people of Israel stood silently, watching. Elijah had no fire in his hand with which to light the wood.

Then he prayed these words: "Answer me, O LORD, answer me, so these people will know that you, O LORD, are God, and that you are turning their hearts back again" (1 Kings 18:37).

That was it! No pleading or shouting or self-mutilation. Just a simple prayer following the restoration of an altar—and the fire of God fell. When it fell, it not only lit the sacrifice, but it "burned up the wood, the stones and the soil, and also licked up the water in the trench" (1 Kings 18:38).

The people repented and returned to God; the prophets of Baal were executed. The hand of the Lord came upon Elijah in such strength that, after praying atop Mount Carmel for an end to the three-and-one-half-year drought, he outran King Ahab's chariot and the brewing storm clouds that held the long-awaited blessing of rain.

That is quite a story! Not only does it tell about a stunning event that happened in ancient Israel, but it also serves as a template for rebuilding our altars and receiving fresh fire.

The Fire of Godly Character

For the fire of God to come, we need to pray according to His will. We also need to walk in integrity of heart, have pure motives and live godly lives.

We have studied the need for rebuilding, which Elijah was keenly aware of, and his preparation for doing the work. There is yet more we can learn. Elijah, as a prophet who stood before God, understood the fire of God as a reflection of His holiness and purity. When we study his life and ministry, it is amazing to see his level of commitment to God and desire to turn the nation to God. Elijah never compromised on his calling.

He also had great understanding of God's covenant and the desperate need we have for true worship. That is why he restored the altar: for worship of our God, the God of Abraham, Isaac and Jacob. He stood firm and did not turn to the popular gods in the nation. No wonder God answered him with fire!

Here are five points of his godly character that are evident in that challenging time—and encourage us in our own trials:

1. Prayer

Elijah was a man of prayer. Although his prophetic work is the most obvious, we must remember that his life's foundation was prayer. The book of James introduces Elijah to us in this way: "Elijah was a man just like us. He prayed earnestly that it would not rain, and it did not rain on the land for three and a half years. Again he prayed, and the heavens gave rain, and the earth produced its crops" (James 5:17–18). Grieved that Israel, under Jezebel's influence, was honoring Baal as the source of their blessings, Elijah started praying earnestly for the Lord to stop the rain in the land, so that Israel might remember that it was not Baal who provided for them, but God. In response to his prayer, the Lord gave Elijah authority to stop rain, to control nature itself.

Elijah lived his life on his knees. That is where his authority came from. God trusts His authority to those He finds on their knees for His glory. With that amazing authority, Elijah went to King Ahab and said, "As the LORD, the God of Israel, lives, whom I serve, there will be neither dew nor rain in the next few years except at my word" (1 Kings 17:1). The phrase *except at my word* shows the level of authority with which God entrusted Elijah. Such standing authority came as the result of time on bended knee. A life of prayer that releases the power of God is the primary qualification we need to restore the altar of God.

The Lord heard Elijah's prayers. When the prophet spoke, the heavens obeyed. God is willing to do the same with us if we are committed to His glory and fire on the altar. God can trust us with authority to do His will when He finds us on our knees. Psalm 8:6 recalls the commission in the Garden where Adam was given authority over nature: "You made him ruler over the works of your hands; you put everything under his feet."

Jesus, who took back the authority Adam lost, gave His disciples authority not only over nature in general, but also over the enemy of righteousness: "He gave them power and authority to drive out all demons and to cure diseases" (Luke 9:1). He said to His disciples, "I have given you authority to trample on snakes and scorpions and to overcome all the power of the enemy; nothing will harm you" (Luke 10:19).

Under such divine authority, we restore or rebuild the altar of God.

2. Humility

After Elijah made his prophecy to Ahab about the drought, after such a great declaration of authority, there was a great test of the prophet's humility: "The word of the LORD came to Elijah: 'Leave here, turn eastward and hide in the Kerith Ravine, east of the Jordan. You will drink from the brook, and I have ordered the ravens to feed you there'" (1 Kings 17:2–4).

The test of the prophet's humility was not simply that God would provide for him by a means he could not control; the greater test was that Elijah would receive bread and meat from the ravens, unclean birds according to Jewish food laws. Elijah learned that authority and humility cannot be separated. The greater the authority, the deeper the humility.

3. *Zeal*

Elijah was driven by zeal for God's name and glory. After the showdown, when Elijah ran from Jezebel and hid in a cave, the Lord came and asked him what he was doing there.

The prophet began his answer with these words: "I have been very zealous for the LORD God Almighty" (1 Kings 19:10). As Elijah continued his answer, he described the spiritual condition of the people of God's covenant. They had neglected and even destroyed the altars of God, turning to idol worship and, as was likely during the drought, even turning on Elijah. By the time the prophet reached the cave, he was convinced he was the only remaining believer in Israel. But Elijah's zeal continued, as did his willingness to pay the price to be a mouthpiece for God.

Throughout Scripture, all of those the Lord used possessed genuine inner zeal for His glory. Nehemiah was zealous for the city and the Israelites. Thus, God used him to reconstruct the walls of Jerusalem. David, when preparing for the construction of the

Temple, was motivated by zeal for the glory of God. God strengthened David's throne and gave him a son who built the Temple and became the wisest and wealthiest of all kings. God used Hezekiah to renovate the Temple and rebuild the destroyed altar because of his zeal for the Lord. The apostles established and built up the Church on a true and strong foundation of the Gospel under great anointing power. Paul in particular possessed zeal for the house and work of God, often reflecting in his letters that his greatest burden was the well-being of the Church. Jesus, in His earthly ministry, was zealous from start to finish: "His disciples remembered that it is written: 'Zeal for your house will consume me'" (John 2:17; see Matthew 21:12–13).

A servant who wants to see God's fire must first be burned with God's love and possess zeal for His glory, name and work.

4. Faith

The psalmist wrote, "Where does my help come from?" Elijah knew it comes from the Lord. At the showdown with the prophets of Baal, "at the time of sacrifice, the prophet Elijah stepped forward and prayed" (1 Kings 18:36). *Step forward* means "draw near, approach, go up." By doing this, Elijah set himself apart. He was demonstrating a life of courage and faith. The Hebrew word we translate as "step forward" is also used for "battle." By faith, Elijah was willing to fight the battle before him. He was willing to be different for the glory of his God.

5. *Patience*

Elijah showed incredible patience. He did not, for instance, just jump into the process of calling down the Lord's fire, tempting as that might have been. He prayed diligently until he received instruction about what to do and the power to do it. Though he had authority to close and open heaven, Elijah obeyed the Lord's word and waited three and a half long years until the right time came to release rain on the land.

The fire of God that precedes the rain of divine blessings comes when God says, not when we say. It cannot be rushed; nor is there a shortcut to bringing it into being. If we step out ahead of God's plans for us, we will not have authority or anointing. We must be willing to wait for the Lord with total commitment. The process of our waiting in obedience is as important to God as repairing the altar and asking for the fire.

The Fire Inside

The Spirit of the Lord is declaring a new season of open gates and opportunities for those who will obey. The first step, building a personal and family altar, should be the focus of every sincere child of God. We need to have a place for the fire of God's love, mercy, grace, life, joy and peace to fall.

When we restore the altar, we focus not on what we can do for God, but on what God has done for us. When the Israelites neglected the altar, they stopped remembering what God had done on their behalf. Whenever they repented of neglecting the altar of God, the next step was to restore it.

That was true in Old Testament times, and it is true today. When the altar of relationship and worship is broken or in ruins, there is no place for the fire of God to burn with lasting impact in our lives or our work for the Kingdom. For individuals, churches and ministries to advance the purposes of God, the fire of God needs to be burning day and night.

We have mentioned that we both love taking teams to nations throughout the earth. The earth is the Lord's and the fullness thereof. Our goal is to keep the fire burning and the remnant encouraged. We want to share with you these words from Marty Cassady, global ambassador in our ministry, describing an experience she had while in Dudley, England:

> As I worshiped and waited in my hotel room for our gathering to begin, I heard the Spirit of the Lord say, *Marty, My fire never rests!* I loved what He was saying and continued to worship and pray that morning. But that evening during worship, the Lord started impressing on me what He was really saying.
>
> First He showed me a picture of Moses in the desert as he turned aside to see the burning bush. Then He showed me the three Hebrew children being thrown into the fiery furnace in Babylon. The next thing He showed me was Elijah in the showdown on Mount Carmel. And finally He showed me the coming of the Holy Spirit in Acts 2.
>
> Since that time I have found many examples of fire in the Word, but what He was showing me specifically was this: *We* are to become His burning ones, altars where the fire never burns out and never rests. His fire today is the same fire that called Moses aside, the same fire that encompassed the three Hebrew children, and the same fire that attested to the one true Living God on Mount Carmel. When Jeremiah complained of his calling, he reached this conclusion: "His

word is in my heart like a fire, a fire shut up in my bones" (Jeremiah 20:9).

I want to decree that you keep the fire burning inside of you and light an altar wherever you go!

Keeping the altar burning wherever we go, being "His burning ones"—this is our goal.

One Final Thing

Before we envelop ourselves further in the true meaning of worship, we want you to evaluate where you are in this process of rekindling the altar fire.

Think honestly: Has your passion for holiness ever waned in the pressure of troubles and difficulties? Has the passage of time shifted your focus to the daily interests of life? Does worship seem like a place that others enter with ease, but with which you struggle?

If it feels as though the fire is burning less brightly on the altar of your heart—or even if it is strong, and you want to keep it that way—take time in this next chapter to realize that it is never too late to turn back to your first love. We will look at a number of examples from Scripture to encourage you to bring back to the altar anything that is missing. Then you will be fully assured for the final chapters, which will prepare you to light an altar wherever you go.

QUESTIONS FOR REFLECTION

1. God's character is, in essence, holiness. Is the fact that God is "a consuming fire" a frightening thought or a comforting thought as you build your altar?
2. What three specific items from the list of altar care instructions in this chapter would best build your relationship with God today? Why?
3. How strong is your faith to believe that God will send fire if you build an altar?

9

Lost Your Way? Go Back!

When we want to restore something, we go back and look at its original design. It is much the same with fire on the altar. When we forget or move away from the original pattern, we lose our passion for holiness. We leave reverence, our holy fear of God, behind. The love, victory, joy and excitement that helped launch our journey of faith are gone. That is when the Spirit of God tells us, "Return to your first love. Go back to the original. Bring back what is missing."

The Way of Return

We read in the Bible about many people who went back to the original to regain the fire of their faith. Here are several examples. See if one of them speaks particularly to your heart.

Jacob Goes Back to Bethel

Bethel, as you recall, was the site of the great encounter Jacob had with God when he saw the ladder stretching to heaven. He was running from his brother, Esau, after stealing the blessing of the birthright. As Jacob traveled through the wilderness, God revealed Himself in a dream, promising that He would prosper and protect Jacob.

The dream was Jacob's first encounter with the God of Abraham and Isaac. He was so taken by this encounter that he made a covenant to come back and build a place of worship for God. He named the place of this encounter *Bethel*, which means "house of God":

> Jacob made a vow, saying, "If God will be with me and will watch over me on this journey I am taking and will give me food to eat and clothes to wear so that I return safely to my father's household, then the LORD will be my God and this stone that I have set up as a pillar will be God's house."
>
> Genesis 28:20–22

The Lord did what He had promised. But like so many of us, Jacob did not. He dwelt in the lowland and allowed the idols of the region into his home. After many years, God spoke once more to Jacob and said, "Go up to Bethel and settle there, and build an altar there to God, who appeared to you when you were fleeing from your brother Esau" (Genesis 35:1). There are two parts to this command.

The first part of the command is for Jacob to go back to the original place of encounter, Bethel. For Jacob, Bethel represented many things about his relationship with God, including a place of divine encounter. Jacob needed to recover his sense of reverence and respect for God who had visited him while he was a fugitive. Bethel was:

- *A Place of Promise*
  God was serious about the promises He had made to Jacob. Returning to Bethel reminded Jacob to be serious about the promises he had made to God.
- *A Place of Destiny*
  At Bethel God had given Jacob an outline of the divine purpose that he was destined to fulfill. Returning to that place would remind Jacob to fulfill God's higher calling.
- *A Place of Inheritance*
  God promised to give Jacob the land where the encounter took place as an inheritance for his descendants.

The second part of God's command to Jacob was to build an altar. After that momentous initial encounter, Jacob had taken the stone he had used as a pillow, set it up as a pillar and poured oil on it with the promise to come back to Bethel, build a house of God and worship. Years had passed, but Jacob had not returned.

After the Lord reminded him of this and commanded him to "build an altar there to God, who appeared to you" (Genesis 35:1), Jacob responded:

Jacob said to his household and to all who were with him, "Get rid of the foreign gods you have with you, and purify yourselves and change your clothes. Then come, let us go up to Bethel, where I will build an altar to God, who answered me in the day of my distress and who has been with me wherever I have gone."

Genesis 35:2–3

Today God is calling us back to Bethel. It is where we rid ourselves of false gods, build the altar of God and offer true worship. Note also that God did not call Jacob back to Bethel simply to visit: He told Jacob to settle and live there. If we truly desire a fresh fire of God, we must go back to the place of revelation and dwell there.

When we go back to dwell in the place of true encounter, God will reveal Himself in a glorious way again as he did for Jacob: "After Jacob returned from Paddan Aram, God appeared to him again and blessed him. God said to him, 'Your name is Jacob, but you will no longer be called Jacob; your name will be Israel.' So he named him Israel" (Genesis 35:9–10).

There are two aspects of beauty in Jacob's story. First, the blessings of God resulted from Jacob's obedience. Because Jacob removed his family idols and returned to Bethel, God blessed him again. These blessings were more than material. They included Jacob's personal transformation and the re-newed understanding of his destiny to fulfill the purposes of God. The goodness of God encompasses both physical and spiritual blessings. Unless we return to our own places of original encounter, no true blessing can result in the lasting fire of revival. We must return to our first love, Jesus Christ.

The second thing of beauty in Jacob's case was that the Lord changed his name. When Jacob returned to Bethel, God gave him a new identity: "Israel," a change that would bring him into his divine destiny. Jacob was given this name before, when he had wrestled with the angel of God and pleaded for God's blessings. At that time God called him "Israel" as a sign of His blessing. But Jacob did not dare to use the name "Israel" in the wrong place. Only upon Jacob's return to worship did he embrace his name of destiny.

One of the main purposes of revival is to bring us into our destinies as members of the Body of Christ. Revival restores our calling as God's children, the Bride of Christ, disciples of and conquerors through the Lord Jesus. In this recovered identity, we can exercise the spiritual authority God has granted us. This is why our return to the heart place or position where we first encountered God through Jesus Christ is so important.

Here are some more examples of the blessing of home-coming.

Naomi Goes Back to Bethlehem

After the loss of her husband and two sons, Naomi decided to go back to Bethlehem for full restoration and greater blessings. Naomi's return also gave her daughter-in-law Ruth the opportunity to live in a new country, know the true God and become part of the lineage of the Lord Jesus Christ.* Naomi's spiritual hunger was only satisfied through her return to Bethlehem, which means "house of bread." The whole city rejoiced when Naomi returned!

David Goes Back to Joy

When King David repented of his sin of adultery with Bathsheba, he prayed, "Restore to me the joy of your salvation and grant me a willing spirit, to sustain me" (Psalm

---

*This has been explored at length in the book *Determination to Make a Difference* (Corinth, Tex.: Gospel of Glory, 2002) by Alemu Beeftu.

51:12). David did not just ask God to forgive his sin; he also asked God to restore to him what he had lost, the joy of his salvation.

That was David's point of homecoming, his return to his first love, his seeking the original fire and passion of his faith. This was also the time when he said to God, "The sacrifices of God are a broken spirit; a broken and contrite heart" (Psalm 51:17). Returning with a broken heart to our original place of holiness and fear of the Lord is the best way to restore the altar for God's fire.

Joseph and Mary Go Back to Jerusalem

According to Luke's gospel, Joseph took his family to Jerusalem every year for the Passover feast. Those first few journeys may have been filled with awe and gratitude for Joseph and Mary to realize that God had chosen them to be responsible for Jesus. They probably felt joy as they fulfilled both the requirement of the Law and their personal responsibilities as parents.

But it is also likely that, over the years and as Jesus grew, this annual journey to Jerusalem became more commonplace and satisfied tradition while offering them a chance to socialize. Maybe Joseph and Mary grew more involved in the social aspect of the journey than its spiritual significance, for they left Jesus behind at the Passover of his twelfth year: "The boy Jesus stayed behind in Jerusalem, but they were unaware of it" (Luke 2:43). In fact, Joseph and Mary traveled back toward home without Jesus all day, assuming that He was with their group.

When Jesus' presence, or His absence, is not noticed in our lives, ministries, churches and homes, that means the fire is gone; the altar is broken. It is time to go back. When Joseph and Mary realized that Jesus was not with them, they hurried back and looked for Him instead of continuing the journey without His presence. They went back to Jerusalem and searched for three days for Jesus until they found Him.

The Only Solution: Go Back!

We have noted that in the book of Revelation the church at Ephesus was rebuked for losing her first love. The Lord commended the people for many good things they did for Him (see Revelation 2:2–3), but those things were not enough without their passionate love for the Lord Jesus Christ. The only solution was to go back: "Remember the height from which you have fallen! Repent and do the things you did at first" (Revelation 2:5).

Committing ourselves to going back, returning to the original pattern, means that we must be concerned first and foremost with a prayerful desire for His Kingdom to come. That is where the authority of the King is fully recognized, manifested and established. When we talk about the Kingdom, we must remember that the heart of the matter is the King. The Kingdom exists for the sake of the King, not vice versa.

God's Will and the Kingdom

It is only as we go back to the original Kingdom pattern that we can understand the will of God and pray and live in accordance with it. The concern we have for the Kingdom moves us to concern for the King. From our concern for the

King, we are moved to be concerned about His will—all that the King would like to see established in His Kingdom.

God's will and purposes span all of time: history, today's world and the new heavens and earth to come. The will of God is not temporary. God's will is eternal, from eternity to eternity. It is not limited by time, but rather continues through time. That is what we are praying when we say the words Jesus taught: *Your Kingdom come, Your will be done.*

God's will is not temporal and neither are our prayers. When we ask something of God, we may be asking Him to accomplish it today, but our prayers are not limited to our circumstances. One thing that weakens the power of prayer is limiting it to our immediate situations. We do need to pray about these things, but we also need to see that, as children of God, our prayers have impact on both the current need and also eternity.

God's will is like that. *Your will be done* speaks to all that God has planned and purposed from eternity past to the distant future. We are accepting and recognizing God's will in the context of His Kingdom. This leads us to the fulfillment of His purposes and overall plans. It also leads us into knowing and understanding the importance of prayer. When we pray, that prayer is part of God's will and His eternal purpose.

As much as we seek to understand the will of God, it is difficult to comprehend fully. That is why the Holy Spirit prays for us. He knows the heart of the Father. He knows the will of the Father. It is why Paul talks about being led by the Holy Spirit. The Holy Spirit prays for us when we do not know how to pray, because our understanding of God's will and His purpose is very limited. We truly do see through a glass darkly.

The Kingdom of God is a kingdom of life. In the context of praying that God's Kingdom or will be done, we are saying we want to go back to life in all of its fullness. We are praying for nothing less than the Christ-life: "I have come that they may have life, and have it to the full" (John 10:10). That is how the Kingdom of God is related to the Great Commission. The Great Commission is to preach the Gospel and disciple others. When we say *Your will be done*, the completion of the Great Commission is included in that prayer.

Jesus said, "I'm not here to do My will, but to do the will of the Father." In Gethsemane He prayed, "It's not My will I seek, but Your will." This shows us that the Kingdom was established through the will of the Father and the obedience of Christ. Jesus gave His life to establish the Kingdom and fulfill the promises of God. When we pray *Your will be done*, we are reaffirming what God wants to do in, through and around us in the Kingdom.

Jesus told His disciples, "I send you just as My Father has sent Me." Jesus came because He was sent by His Father; and He lived for the will of the Father. As Jesus lived for the Father's will, we too are called to live for His Father's will. That is why aligning our prayers with God's will is so vital. His will and our prayers affect the coming of the Kingdom.

And what is more, knowing God's will is part of the blessing He intends for us on earth. What a blessing it is to know God's will in our walks with Him and when fellowshiping with Him! Knowing God's will every day and walking in obedience to it is the greatest blessing a human can enjoy. We echo Jesus' heart in our own willingness to serve: "Here I am. As it is written, I came to do Your will."

Our days were recorded in God's Book of Life before we even came into existence (see Psalm 139:16). By praying *Your will be done*, we are agreeing with what is already recorded in God's book. We are saying that we choose to go back: to submit our will, accept His agenda and follow Him, wherever He leads. We find that it is a blessing to go back, for His will brings blessings to our lives and glory to His name.

The Mystery of God's Will

In Ephesians 1:9, Paul tells us that God revealed the mystery of His will to His children. It is possible for God's children to know the will of God. How? Through the Word of God, the Holy Spirit and God's anointing upon us. The main reason we are able to know God's will, however, is that He wants us to know His will. He has put us on earth to fulfill His will. Hear Jesus' words again: "I have sent you as My Father has sent Me." When God, as a good Father and Shepherd, sends us, therefore, He is not going to hide His will from us. It is a joy for the Lord to reveal His will to His children because it builds our relationships with Him.

When we pray *Your will be done*, we are saying, "I am willing to carry out Your desires." When we pray and ask God to reveal His will, purpose and plan to us, it indicates a willingness to follow. This also means that we are willing to pay the price. Rest assured, there is always a price to pay in order to fulfill God's will. There is a cost for submission and obedience. Are we willing to pay the price for the fulfillment of the Lord's will?

When we say *Your will be done*, God's grace is manifested. God does not tell His children to go and accomplish His will alone. God does not work that way. Whenever we say yes to His will, God's grace is released. Every time we say yes to God's will, no matter how heavy or difficult the burden may be, the grace of God is released, bringing power for what we are facing.

We see this in the lives of Peter and John and the other believers, as recorded in Acts 4 not long after Pentecost. When they purposed to preach the Gospel in spite of the prohibition of the Sanhedrin, God released an overflow of His sufficient grace and mighty power. God blessed their willing hearts and the Kingdom was strengthened: "After they prayed, the place where they were meeting was shaken. And they were all filled with the Holy Spirit and spoke the word of God boldly" (Acts 4:31).

Going back to the original Kingdom design and pattern—shown clearly in the second chapter of Acts—is the only way to ignite the fire of revival in our hearts. Going back to the original plan and purposes of God for our lives within the Kingdom is the number one key to a true spiritual awakening that brings lasting transformation.

In order to go back to the original, we need to know where we are in our relationship with God and where He would like us to be. If you have any conviction that the fire is lessening on the altar of your heart, then God's question for you is: "Where are you?" As you answer this question by praying, "Your Kingdom come, Your will be done," then you will experience the full manifestation of God's grace for fruitfulness and an extraordinary relationship with Him for abundant life.

QUESTIONS FOR REFLECTION

1. Which of the stories from Scripture about going back to the original pattern means the most to you? Why?

2. In your view, what is the relationship between the will of God and the Kingdom of God?

3. As a child of God, when you say *Your Kingdom come, and Your will be done*, what does that mean for you? How does that describe your relationship with the Lord?

10

Lord, Return the Fire to the Altar!

Restoring an altar of true worship results in lasting Kingdom activity where people are being saved, delivered and healed on every level. From the spiritual to the intellectual, the abundant, thriving life is now possible as we are empowered to live in a way that radiates the glory of God.

We need a paradigm shift in the way we think about the altar, specifically the altar of worship. Typically, the altar of worship is viewed as a time of family devotions, personal prayer and study of the Word, along with a weekly church service with spiritual songs and a spiritual lesson. Yet if we are serious about fire on the altar, that concept needs to change. True worship is not limited to a specific place and time.

Do you agree or disagree with the following statement? *Worship is a ministry to which every child of God is called.* If, in fact, that is the case, we need to change our view of worship altogether. Worship is much more than what we might do on any given Sunday, or at specific times in our homes. Ministry is so much more than the Christian activities we engage in during the week until we go to church on Sunday. Worship and ministry are one and the same, and any attempt to dissect the two ends up doing what dissection usually does: It kills. Every person's call to ministry is to exalt and lift up the name of the Lord every moment, everywhere. That is what true worship is all about.

Worship is encountering the holy Living God and giving Him adoration and the sacrifice of praise in response to His goodness. This also implies pouring out our hearts in reverence before Him. If this is worship, how do we worship? How do we come into the presence of God?

What Worship Is Not—and What It Is

Worship is often wrongly defined. In worship services, we follow various styles or forms of expression including songs, praise and adoration. People who stand up and sing believe that is what true worship is. Those who raise their hands think they are worshiping. People performing a holy dance before the Lord feel that is worship. Biblically speaking, none of these is worship; these are expressions of worship.

Sincere worship is encountering the Holy God. In that encounter we come to understand His holiness, purity, majesty and character. We become reverent and recognize that He alone is worthy to receive our praise, adoration and worship. The form or style of worship is not important; standing, dancing, raising our hands or singing does not define "true" worship, but only worship's expression.

What is important is the reason for worship. The issue is not how we sing, but why we sing. The *why* makes worship acceptable or not acceptable to God. If worship is based on our encounters with the Lord, this may mean that sometimes we have nothing to say; we are silent. John, for example, saw Jesus walking among the churches described in Revelation 1. He started looking at Jesus from head to foot, at His majesty, power and glory. Soon John was on his face like a dead man. Was that worship? Yes.

Those who define worship as shouting and dancing, or otherwise being demonstrative, may not recognize John's stillness and silence as worship, but it was. What about when David brought back the Ark of God and jumped before the Lord with all his might? Was that worship? Yes.

Who displayed true worship? David or John? Both! Neither of the men worshiped with a predetermined style or form. Both worshiped in a unique and individual way that was a natural response to his reason for worshiping—his awe, joy and understanding of who God is.

John, in his revelation, saw Jesus face-to-face; he did not have the strength to stand or jump. David had experienced the promises of God and the covenant, and the Ark of the Covenant was coming. His joy expressed itself in jumping.

Worship is our genuine, wholehearted response to a holy, almighty God. There is no formula for worship, since true worship can and should happen at any moment, anywhere. This is part of the paradigm shift we must embrace concerning worship and the altar of God. Our focus on personal renewal—the restoring of our hearts to our Creator—must begin with a core issue: worship. The altar of worship is the foundation of covenant relationship with God.

True Worship Reflects God's Glory

In true worship, we focus on God with the fervent desire to see His glory and reflect it in our daily lives. Glorifying God in everything we do is the call of every child of God. This is what God's Word encourages in 1 Corinthians 10:31: "So whether you eat or drink or whatever you do, do it all for the glory of God." We can only do everything for the glory of God when our focus is to honor Him. Paul further defines this process by saying: "We, who with unveiled faces all reflect the Lord's glory, are being transformed into his image with ever-increasing glory, which comes from the Lord, who is the Spirit" (2 Corinthians 3:18).

When we do everything in order to reflect His glory instead of trying to highlight our gifts or abilities, true worship is the result. The altar that reflects God's glory in everything by the power of the Holy Spirit is restored for the fresh fire of lasting revival. True worship brings us closer to God and gives the Holy Spirit freedom to change us into the people we need to be. We bring honor to God and become more like Jesus in the process.

The call of God is to a relationship with a living Savior. Jesus established a relationship with the disciples before He sent them out with authority (see Mark 3:13–14). In the same way, our worship and service to God originate in the relationship we have with Christ. Your relationship and fellowship with God provide the basic foundation of worship that pleases Him.

I, Alemu, have two children, the older being a girl. When she was four or five years of age, most mornings she would come quietly into my prayer room to be with me as I prayed. I am usually on my face before the Lord during my private prayer time. So, my daughter would lie down on my back while I prayed. A few times, I stopped praying to ask her if she wanted to go back to sleep.

Every time I asked her that question, her response was the same. "No, Dad. I know you're praying. I won't bother you. I just want to be with you."

Whenever my daughter spoke those words, the Lord reminded me that the desire of His heart is for me to do the same with Him; just come into His presence saying, "Dad, I just want to be with You and fellowship with You."

God's desire and plan for our lives is for us to be changed into the likeness of Christ. Jesus did not die for activities like so much "ministry" we see among Christians today; Jesus paid the price so we can be His children. Paul told the believers in Rome that this was the preplan of God for their lives: "Those God foreknew he also predestined to be conformed to the likeness of his Son, that he might be the firstborn among many brothers" (Romans 8:29).

Changing into the likeness of Christ, by the plan of God the Father and the work of the Holy Spirit, is a result of a daily relationship with God. Without this true relationship, there is no worship or ministry. But where there is true relationship, there is true worship. The process of fire on the altar begins at this point, with individual believers and their Kingdom communities experiencing newness of mind, the power of the Holy Spirit and the full revelation of the Word of God.

The Fire of Obedience

Our worship is demonstrated through wholehearted obedience to God's will and purpose. Indeed, the only way to honor God and express our true love for Him is by obeying Him. Obedience requires total submission to God and determination to fulfill His purpose. That is why obedience is better than sacrifice in God's eyes. Remember Samuel's words: "Does the LORD delight in burnt offerings and sacrifices as much as in obeying the voice of the LORD? To obey is better than sacrifice, and to heed is better than the fat of rams" (1 Samuel 15:22). True worship begins not by bringing things to God, but by presenting ourselves to Him. Obedience involves one's heart, will, strength and soul. True worship involves one's total being. Something less may look like worship, but it is not.

Understanding worship means understanding obedience. Obedience to God is more than an emotional response to music or a moving message. It always involves some measure of sacrifice. That is why it was so painful for Jesus to go to the cross. Philippians 2:8 indicates that Jesus fulfilled the will of His Father through obedience, in humility of attitude and purity of heart: "He humbled himself and became obedient to death—even death on a cross!" Obedience in humility is a sure foundation for worship.

The essence of fire on the altar is worshiping God with an obedient and humble heart. He desires for us to restore the true humility that enables us to glorify Him in everything we do, day and night, like the 24 elders who "fall down before him who sits on the throne, and worship him who lives for ever and ever. They lay their crowns before the throne" (Revelation 4:10).

Fire on the altar for a fresh fire of revival begins here. True worship makes the will of God the center of everything. There can be no true obedience if we do not know the will of God.

Living for His will starts by knowing His will. Jesus did not just say, "I obey My Father." He said, "Here I am, to do your will, O God, just as it is written of me in the book of the Law" (Hebrews 10:7 GNT). Even facing the cross, His words were, "I want your will to be done, not mine" (Matthew 26:39 NLT). When Paul received his calling, he was told that the God of his fathers had chosen him to know His will (see Acts 22:14). Fire on the altar for a fresh fire of revival begins, therefore, with knowing the will of God for our personal lives and obediently fulfilling that will.

In Your Upper Room

Scripture provides a picture to help us understand this place of worship in our hearts, the center of hearing and knowing God's will. It is the "upper room"—a place of meditation, prayer, worship and seeking the Lord. This room with a view into the plans and purposes of God is necessary for us if we desire to see God's fire fall.

Upper rooms in Scripture were cool, comfortable summer rooms used to receive company and hold celebrations. Kings used upper rooms or upper chambers to display their luxurious wealth or glory (see Judges 3:23; 2 Kings 23:12). There was an upper room in the Temple (see 1 Chronicles 28:11; 2 Chronicles 3:9). It served as a symbol for the point of origin of God's blessings:

> He waters the mountains from His upper rooms; the earth is satisfied and abounds with the fruit of His works. He causes vegetation to grow for the cattle, and all that the earth produces for man to cultivate, that he may bring forth food out of the earth.
>
> Psalm 104:13–14 AMPC

It was a special place to commune with God, hear His voice and experience His power. This is the reason Elijah brought the body of the widow's son into the upper room. He heard the Lord in that room. He knew the Lord would hear his cry, and sure enough, "the LORD heard Elijah's cry, and the boy's life returned to him, and he lived" (1 Kings 17:22). Most likely, that upper room is where Elijah heard the voice of God tell him to go and reveal himself to King Ahab. This is where he discerned the timing of God and changing of that season. Upper rooms were used by the prophets for worship, prayer, intercession, hearing the voice of God, and receiving guidance and messages for the people they served.

Maybe the upper room for you is an actual room in your house or workplace, a place of quiet rest near to the heart of God. Maybe the upper room is not a literal collection of wood and brick, but a special place in the heart, a place you go to when you desire to hear the voice of God and receive His touch.

The Upper Room most familiar to us is, of course, the place where the Lord Jesus celebrated the Last Supper:

> He sent two of his disciples, telling them, "Go into the city, and a man carrying a jar of water will meet you. Follow him. Say to the owner of the house he enters, 'The Teacher asks: Where is my guest room, where I may eat the Passover with my disciples?' He will show you a large upper room, furnished and ready. Make preparations for us there." The disciples left, went into the city and found things just as Jesus had told them. So they prepared the Passover.
>
> Mark 14:13–16; see Luke 22:12

The Upper Room was a place where Jesus could bring closure to His ministry of teaching. Furthermore, the Upper

Room for Christ was a place of surrender to the will of His Father. In the Upper Room Jesus showed His disciples the true nature of servanthood by washing their feet. Note that as Jesus washed the disciples' feet, He did not say anything about their spiritual condition. In fact, later that night Peter would deny Him three times. Judas had already sold Jesus into the hands of the Sanhedrin and was just waiting for the right time to betray Him with an insincere kiss. But Jesus washed their feet, nonetheless. An upper room worship experience with God can bring about surrender to Him and death to pride and self, resulting in a servant's heart—something desperately needed in our generation.

After Jesus' resurrection and ascension, it is probable that that same Upper Room was the place where the disciples waited upon the Lord to receive the promise of the Holy Spirit: "When they arrived [in Jerusalem from the Mount of Olives], they went upstairs to the room where they were staying. . . . They all joined together constantly in prayer. . . . When the day of Pentecost came, they were all together in one place" (Acts 1:13–14, 2:1). The Holy Spirit would transform the frightened disciples into bold witnesses empowered to take the Gospel to all nations.

The disciples needed a place of unity, prayer, waiting and then receiving power to do the work of God. For them, as for us, it would be hard to experience any of these without an upper room in which to hear God's voice and wait for His fire to fall.

Going Forth in Power

When the disciples went forth, filled with the Holy Spirit, they maintained service to God with pure hearts. Likewise, we serve the Lord—maintaining right motives—not by our own power but the power of the Holy Spirit.

Like the apostles' call in the New Testament, the call of the priest in the Old Testament was to serve God and teach the people of God how to live holy lives. King Hezekiah, during the purification of the Temple, appealed to the priests by saying, "My sons, do not be negligent now, for the LORD has chosen you to stand before him and serve him, to minister before him and to burn incense" (2 Chronicles 29:11).

This gives us an important key to living at the altar of worship. The drawing in chapter 7 showed us the physical layout of the Tabernacle, with the altar of bronze at the entrance where the priests laid out the sacrifices and the fire fell, and the golden altar of incense in the Holy Place, on which the priests burned fragrant incense on coals taken from the altar of bronze.

What does priestly order in an ancient building of worship have to do with our lives now? Paul gives us the answer: "Do you not know that your body is a temple of the Holy Spirit, who is in you, whom you have received from God? You are not your own; you were bought at a price. Therefore honor God with your body" (1 Corinthians 6:19–20).

When Moses built the Tabernacle, he built everything, not just the altar. It was the same with Solomon and the Temple. Under both Hezekiah (see 2 Chronicles 29) and Josiah (see 2 Kings 22), the priests repaired and purified not only the altar, but also the whole Temple of God.

We must see that in order to have lives of service to God, in order to come with pure hearts to the altar of worship, we must devote every area of our lives to Him, not only one area that we call "worship." Everything about us should bring honor and glory to God, since the blood of Christ that was shed for us on the cross, the true altar, purchases us.

Starting from the Day of Pentecost, believers have become the temple of God, the place where the fire of God will fall. As temples, as the dwelling place of God, we should glorify Him in everything we do, with pure hearts and clear consciences and sincere faith.

This means dealing obediently with everyday issues, the trials and frustrations of day-to-day life. This is how we maintain proper order. Only when everything is in its place according to the divine order can God light our sacrifices of praise with His fire. He looks at our hearts and motives before our sacrifices. When everything is in divine order, God accepts our worship.

The natural outflow of having everything in divine order is seeing His Kingdom come, His will accomplished. We want things on earth to be as they are in heaven. Our prayer that *Your Kingdom come* is a prayer to establish the Lordship of Jesus Christ. It assumes His authority as Creator, Father, Redeemer, Ruler and King of kings; we see all in relation to Kingdom power. *Your Kingdom come* reflects the character and power of the Kingdom of God; in other words, the Gospel. The Kingdom of God is the Kingdom of forgiveness and salvation. It is a Kingdom where He makes all things new.

That is definitely Good News! In the next chapter, we will explore the Kingdom values we are called to share.

QUESTIONS FOR REFLECTION

1. In your own words, describe true worship in one or two sentences.

2. What are the signs that let you know your life is in order?

3. Why do you suppose order in the Tabernacle and Temple was so crucial to the proper worship of God?

11

Understanding God's Kingdom

As God begins to move, our prayer and worship at the altar cannot be disassociated from Kingdom work. The ultimate purpose and plan of God is the salvation of people. Jesus said, "All authority has been given to Me on earth; therefore, go." The authority of the Kingdom establishes the Kingdom.

Praying for God's Kingdom to come involves welcoming the values of that Kingdom. The values of the Kingdom of heaven are different from those of the kingdom of man. Where there is a human kingdom, the attention inevitably focuses on human things.

A recurring challenge for believers is to make the distinction between building personal kingdoms and building the Kingdom of God. In the spiritual context of ministry, we can be so involved in activities or in building our personal kingdoms that we forget the King. When we become overwhelmed and involved in our kingdoms, we become little kings and possibly even little tyrants. We must be diligent in resisting this temptation, for the fruit it produces centers around turf rather than the Kingdom—the question becomes, How large is *my* territory, *my* ruling area?

But Jesus taught, "If you exalt My name, then focus on My Kingdom. Say: '*Your* Kingdom come!'"

When we are committed to the Kingdom of Jesus, we can sincerely pray, "Your Kingdom come." When we submit to the authority of the King, we are accepting His total authority. By saying *Your Kingdom come*, we lay down our aspirations or goals for our personal kingdoms at the foot of the cross and leave them there.

Praying *Your Kingdom come* also brings forth the manifestations and characteristics of that Kingdom. Everything God wants to do in this world until Jesus returns is done through the Kingdom. John the Baptizer started his preaching ministry by declaring, "The Kingdom of God is here. The Kingdom of God has come." Later on, Jesus talked about the Kingdom being at hand. Today, everything God does is accomplished in the context of His Kingdom.

Since this is the case, our worship at the altar leads to our lives of service to God in His Kingdom. What are some of the major characteristics of the Kingdom of God? What are the Kingdom issues? What are some of the key elements to keep in mind, particularly when we pray, "Your Kingdom come"? How do we live for the Kingdom?

The Kingdom Is Characterized by Life

The essence of the Kingdom is life. In John 3 we see Nicodemus, a teacher of the Jews, coming to Jesus at night saying,

"No one could perform the miraculous signs you are doing if God were not with him" (verse 2).

But Jesus told Nicodemus he was missing the point: The point was not to admire the miracles. The point was to understand that unless you are born again, you will not see the Kingdom of God. The Kingdom of God is life.

The Great Commission is very important in the context of understanding that the Kingdom of God is a kingdom of life. Whether we pray, fast or worship, we must come back to the purpose of the Kingdom, which is life. Jesus said, "I came that you may have life and have it abundantly." There are those who do not know the Lord and those who do know Him and need to be discipled—both are important in the Kingdom of God. It is the reason He said to go and make disciples.

The Kingdom Is Characterized by Lordship

The Lordship of Jesus Christ is the foundation of the Kingdom of God. At the time of Jesus' birth, the wise men asked, "Where is the King of the Jews?" They knew about the Kingdom of God—in fact, they had been waiting for it—and they were looking for its King. They were asking for the King in order to submit to His lordship. Furthermore, as we have noted, Paul talks about this in Philippians 2:8–11, explaining that Jesus humbled Himself. As a result, God the Father exalted Him and gave Him the name above every name. This indicates the authority of Jesus Christ. God the Father exalted Him, so He is King and Lord.

Revelation 17:14 says that Jesus is "Lord of lords and King of kings." Jesus Christ is not a king or a lord, but rather *the* Lord of lords and *the* King of kings. He is the ultimate authority and ultimate ruler. When we say *Your Kingdom come*, we are saying we accept His lordship. We bow down before His lordship and submit to His authority.

The challenge for those of us who accept the lordship of Jesus and enter the Kingdom of God is to demonstrate by our lives and walks that we sincerely desire the Kingdom to come. Then our main questions must be, Is Jesus Lord of my work? Is He Lord of my activities? Is He Lord of my plans and dreams? Is He Lord of my business? Is He Lord of my church? Is He Lord of my desires, property, possessions, gifts, talents, title, past, present and future? Is He the Lord of all? When we say *Your Kingdom come*, we are saying that we want Jesus to be Lord of all!

The first thing that must be recognized when His Kingdom is established is that He is Lord over everything. That is why it is so challenging, even after praying that His Kingdom will come, actually to walk in the Kingdom. Without accepting His lordship and recognizing that He is the Lord, we number ourselves among those working against the Kingdom. And that is a losing position, because His Kingdom will come.

The Kingdom Is Characterized by Forgiveness

A vital component of our Lord's ministry was forgiveness. The purpose of preaching repentance is that it leads to forgiveness. The Old Testament prophets who foretold the Messiah looked forward to the coming Kingdom of God and invited the Israelites to repent. The essence of Jesus' message was repentance and forgiveness. John the Baptist preached repentance when he came to prepare the way: "Repent and turn, for the Kingdom is coming."

When the King comes, there is life, authority and forgiveness of sins. God is clearly interested in the forgiveness of sins. Jesus illustrated this during His early teachings when they brought a woman for Him to condemn. He said, "I forgive you and am not going to condemn you" (see John 8:11). He was moved not by anger or judgment but by compassion, and forgiveness was the natural result. Later, as He went to the cross, Jesus pleaded with the Father to forgive His killers: "Father, forgive them, for they don't know what they are doing." That was His cry even in the context of their rejection, torture and ultimate death-dealing.

If we asked Jesus why He did this, His simple answer would be, "My Kingdom is the Kingdom of forgiveness. That's why I'm giving My life. That's why I'm shedding My blood." Jesus' prayer on the cross was a verbalization of His entire life.

Why? Because the Kingdom of God is the Kingdom of forgiveness. Jesus practiced this throughout His earthly life. Romans 5:8 says that Jesus died for us while we were still sinners. Even today, Jesus stands at the right hand of the Father and intercedes for us. When we say *Your Kingdom come*, therefore, we must understand that the Kingdom of God cannot be established without forgiveness. A common hindrance to keeping the fire burning at the altar is an unforgiving attitude. If we say "Lord, Lord" without true and sincere forgiveness, it is ineffective. The Kingdom of Jesus forgives and is characterized by forgiveness.

The Kingdom Is Characterized by Jesus' Will

The Kingdom and the will of the Lord cannot be separated. *Your Kingdom come* and *Your will be done* are spoken in succession in the Lord's Prayer for a reason. *Your will be done* is discussed further in the next chapter.

The Kingdom Is Characterized by Power

The Kingdom of God encompasses the power to save, redeem, change, transform and deliver. It is a kingdom of power, not discussion. Paul refers to this in 1 Corinthians 4:20: "For the kingdom of God is not a matter of talk but of power." God has always wanted His people to know this. Even in the Old Testament, the prophet Isaiah spoke forth this message: "You who are far away, hear what I have done; you who are near, acknowledge my power!" (Isaiah 33:13). God was telling the Israelites of His nature. He invited those who did not know Him to consider His power, which would lead them to the Good News of salvation.

The Kingdom of God is a kingdom of power, and this power is available to His children. The people of the Kingdom are overcomers because of this power. God's power is available to forgive, love, deliver, bring the Good News and face challenges. Paul refers to our victory by the wonderful phrase *We are more than conquerors*. After Jesus promised the coming of the Holy Spirit, He told His followers to stay in Jerusalem until they received the Holy Spirit. When the Holy Spirit came upon them, they received power.

Remember that the Kingdom of God is based on a particular kind of power—the power of the resurrection. After the resurrection, God the Father gave Jesus the name that is above all names, the Lord, and all power and authority both in the heavens and on the earth.

Through His resurrection, Jesus established the power of the Kingdom. His power makes it possible for us to put the temples of our bodies in order, to restore our altars, to receive the fire of God. He overcame the power of death, sin and all hindrances that keep us from coming into relationship with the Father. It is impossible, therefore, to separate the Kingdom of God from the miracle-working power of God. Paul referred to this in his letter to the Romans:

> I glory in Christ Jesus in my service to God. I will not venture to speak of anything except what Christ has accomplished through me in leading the Gentiles to obey God by what I have said and done—by the power of signs and miracles, through the power of the Spirit.
>
> Romans 15:17–19

Paul was talking about the reality of the Kingdom. He was preaching the Gospel of the Kingdom. That is why the power of the Kingdom was manifested in his works. Even at the beginning of the disciples' preaching, according to Mark 16:20, they "went out and preached everywhere, and the Lord worked with them and confirmed his word by the signs that accompanied it." That is the power of the Kingdom! Jesus confirmed His Word, the Gospel of the Kingdom, through signs and wonders as they preached.

In Acts, chapter 4, we read of the time the disciples were ordered to stop preaching the Gospel. Their response was a prayer that looked back into history and acknowledged God's power over all:

> "Sovereign Lord," they said, "you made the heaven and the earth and the sea, and everything in them. You spoke by the Holy Spirit through the mouth of your servant, our father David, 'Why do the nations rage and the peoples plot in vain?

The kings of the earth take their stand . . . against the Lord and against his Anointed One.'"

Acts 4:24–26

Then they asked God to reveal His power, the power of His Kingdom, once again so they could continue to preach the Gospel:

"Now, Lord, consider their threats and enable your servants to speak your word with great boldness. Stretch out your hand to heal and perform miraculous signs and wonders through the name of your holy servant Jesus."

Acts 4:29–30

The disciples knew the Kingdom of God was established by the power of the Holy Spirit and asked for the power they were entitled to have. The same power is available to you and me.

The Kingdom Is Characterized by Love

"For God so loved the world that he gave his one and only Son" (John 3:16). God's Son came because of love, and the Kingdom was then established upon that love. Everything God does is based upon His love. Faith, hope and love last forever, but the greatest of these is love. Love is the most excellent way. After sharing with the Corinthians about the gift of the Holy Spirit, Paul told them, "Eagerly desire the greater gifts. And now I will show you the most excellent way" (1 Corinthians 12:31). The most excellent way is the way of love.

First Corinthians 13 reflects the Kingdom standard of love. Paul said, "If I do all these things and don't have love,

I am nothing." If we say we are people of the Kingdom but fail to show love, we reveal that the truth is not in us. If we pray, sing and serve in all areas of ministry, but do not have love, we are not in the Kingdom because the Kingdom of Jesus is characterized by love. Love is the reason Jesus instructed us to pray, "Your Kingdom come."

Christ relates to us through love, calls to us through love and forgives us because of love. The entire letter that we know as 1 John teaches this clearly: "Dear friends, let us love one another, for love comes from God. . . . No one has ever seen God; but if we love one another, God lives in us and his love is made complete in us" (1 John 4:7, 12).

The Kingdom Is Characterized by Unity

The Kingdom of God is a kingdom of unity. There is unity in the Kingdom, because there is just one true King. All others are His servants who walk with Him, do His will and accomplish His purposes.

Jesus prayed for the unity of believers; for oneness (see John 17:21). Let them be one, He said, because they are in the Kingdom and under the authority of the King. Paul referred to this when he urged believers to keep the unity of the Spirit. When a person enters the Kingdom, he becomes part of this unity. We are not called to create unity but to keep the unity purchased for us at the price of Jesus' death and resurrection (see Ephesians 2).

The Kingdom Is Characterized by Light

The Word became flesh and dwelt among us; the Light of the world, overcoming the darkness. He established His

Kingdom, and now those who were in darkness, in the shadow of death, have hope because of the Light. We can see life, hope, joy and victory because of the Light. And that Light is Christ in us.

Jesus said that the people of the Kingdom not only live in the light, but also are the light of the world. He gave His children the authority to act and shine as the light. All through the New Testament, we are encouraged to let our light shine.

The Kingdom implication is that our walks with the Lord are to be pure and revelatory, hiding nothing under a bushel, but displaying our lives for all to see. We are invited to walk in the light, particularly in our prayer lives. True worship at the altar cannot take place without walking in the light.

His Kingdom Is Characterized by Peace

Jesus' peace is infinite shalom. He is the Prince of peace, and since the Kingdom is the Kingdom of Jesus Christ, He is the King of peace. When He rules our lives and hearts, the peace of Jesus flows like a river. We bask in the peace of the Lord. The greatest promise Jesus gave His disciples was this: the promise of the Holy Spirit, the promise that the Comforter would come. He gives peace, but not as the world gives peace.

When we say *Your Kingdom come*, we have the responsibility to exhibit His peace—with God, others and ourselves. If we are in the Kingdom and practice peace, we are people who are known as peacemakers: "Blessed are the peacemakers, for they will be called sons of God" (Matthew 5:9).

The Kingdom Is Characterized by Blessings

Jesus said, "Seek first [God's] kingdom and his righteousness, and all these things will be given to you as well" (Matthew 6:33). The Kingdom of God is a kingdom of blessings. We see this clearly in creation. After creating male and female, He brought them together and blessed them. The first communication between God and created human beings was a blessing.

The blessing of God is not manifested only through material things, but also through the joy, peace and forgiveness of the Lord. God's blessing encompasses many areas. It is everything that comes from the Lord, whether it is physical, spiritual, emotional or intellectual. It is completeness in Christ Jesus. When we worship at the altar we are, therefore, bold to pray, "Lord, Your Kingdom come."

QUESTIONS FOR REFLECTION

1. What is the most important step in entering the Kingdom of God? Can you describe when you took that step?
2. What is the purpose of the Kingdom of God?
3. How do we receive blessings from the Kingdom of God?

12

Rekindle Your Prayer Fire

The fire of God that comes by prayer can be kept alive only by prayer. One day, after Jesus returned from praying, His disciples made a request: "Lord, teach us to pray, just as John taught his disciples" (Luke 11:1). It appears this appeal was based on the disciples' struggles at a personal level. They witnessed Jesus praying on a regular basis, whether going out to the desert early in the morning, praying all night or going to the mountain to pray. His example fueled their desire.

Their appeal was right, and Jesus capitalized on it. They did not say, "Lord, teach us how to preach." Neither did they ask how to be disciples or how to plant churches. What they desired was training in prayer. They saw Jesus' direct communication with His Father, and that He would not do anything without first talking to Him. His relationship with the Father and the Holy Spirit through prayer was what the disciples noticed and wanted.

Another probable reason they asked Jesus to teach them to pray was that they saw the Pharisees and religious leaders praying in order to impress people. Jesus told them not to do as the Pharisees did: "When you pray, do not be like the hypocrites, for they love to pray standing in the synagogues and on the street corners to be seen by men" (Matthew 6:5). The Pharisees clearly prayed and fasted for public display, not because of any relationship with God.

Jesus' life exemplified the way He prayed. Jesus' disciples saw His sincerity. They saw His consistency and commitment to prayer. The disciples saw that Jesus' prayer life was real, and that is what they sought.

Now, because the disciples often struggled in their humanness, they might have thought that Jesus was going to give them a methodology for prayer. In all likelihood, they were looking for a process they could go through and feel satisfied after completion. That would be like looking for the *how* rather than the *why*. But what they really needed was the *why*. And the answer to the *why* of prayer was the meaningful relationship with the Father that Jesus had.

The foundation of effective prayer that brings divine fire is the passion to pursue relationship.

The Essential Aspects of Prayer

Jesus taught His disciples five essential aspects of prayer: 1) understanding the reason for prayer; 2) being consistent in prayer; 3) fulfilling our responsibilities in prayer; 4) understanding the faithfulness of God; and 5) understanding the power of God.

1. *Understanding the Reason for Prayer*

Jesus did not go stand on a street corner to pray; He went in solitude to the desert. His disciples probably marveled at this because it was not what they were used to seeing. Why did He not go to public places so people could watch and admire Him? Why not position Himself so people would say, "Wow! He's intelligent and fantastic!"

No, Jesus did not do this. In many ways it was expected that He should, but Jesus was not bound by the expectations of others. Why would Jesus not pray as others prayed?

Jesus gave the answer in Mathew 6:5: "I tell you the truth, they have received their reward in full." The Pharisees were praised by the crowds for their "piety" and, therefore, received their reward in human admiration. This was little more than paganism, and Jesus said His disciples should not be like the pagans:

> "When you pray, go into your room, close the door and pray to your Father, who is unseen. Then your Father, who sees what is done in secret, will reward you. And when you pray, do not keep on babbling like pagans, for they think they will be heard because of their many words."
>
> Matthew 6:6–7

The most crucial factor in prayer is to make a distinction between ritual and relationship. Prayer is a meaningful relationship, not a form of religion. Jesus did not use this opportunity to tell His disciples *how* to pray; rather He wanted to focus their intentions on *why* to pray. He said, "When you pray, pray to your Father."

Unless we understand relationship, we cannot pray. Without relationship, we are simply performing a religious exercise.

This was the reason He went to pray in the desert rather than in the synagogue. He was not interested in positive reviews for public piety.

Being rewarded and admired does not matter. A person's relationship with the Father is the critical factor. The significance of going into a private place and closing the door is to avoid everything that is distracting, including one's desire to impress others.

2. Being Consistent in Prayer

The second essential aspect of prayer is consistency. When the reason for praying is established, *why* you pray is much easier to explain.

Why do I pray? I want to relate to God the Father, Son and Holy Spirit on a personal level. I want to relate to my Creator, Redeemer and Comforter. I want this to be the priority.

In a relationship, consistency cannot be overemphasized. The reason Jesus prayed in the desert or on the mountain was because of His relationship with the Father, a relationship He did not want to neglect. Because He was committed to it, He spent time to maintain and develop it. Paul underlined the same concept: "Be unceasing in prayer [praying perseveringly]" (1 Thessalonians 5:17 AMPC).

3. Fulfilling Our Responsibilities in Prayer

Jesus told the disciples a parable about a man who went to a friend's house at midnight asking for bread. At first the needy man was refused by his sleepy friend; but his persistence finally convinced his friend to meet his need (see Luke 11:5–8). This story shows that our human responsibility in prayer has two aspects:

- What is required first is our recognition of relationship with the one we go to in prayer. The man who needed bread went to his friend on the basis of their relationship, even at the inconvenient time of midnight.

- Second, once we recognize that relationship as the basis of prayer, we must be persistent about it. Persistence strengthens the relationship and results in answered prayer.

Praying is active; therefore, we take the responsibility to seek God. We also accept the responsibility to keep at it and not give up. Accepting our responsibility enables us to be engaged in prayer proactively with commitment, diligence and determination.

4. *Understanding the Faithfulness of God*

The fourth essential aspect of prayer that Jesus talked about is the faithfulness of God. He asked the disciples these questions:

> "Which of you fathers, if your son asks for a fish, will give him a snake instead? Or if he asks for an egg, will give him a scorpion? If you then, though you are evil, know how to give good gifts to your children, how much more will your Father in heaven give the Holy Spirit to those who ask him!"
>
> Luke 11:11–13

Prayer does not depend on our human faithfulness as much as on God's faithfulness. God is faithful to inspire and enable us to pray, through the Holy Spirit, as well as to hear and answer our prayers. We must understand the faithfulness of God as we pray. He is the One who promised, "Call to me and I will answer you and tell you great and unsearchable things you do not know" (Jeremiah 33:3).

5. *Understanding the Power of God*

Jesus wanted to help the disciples understand the power of the Holy Spirit: "If you then, though you are evil, know how to give good gifts to your children, how much more will your Father in heaven give the Holy Spirit to those who ask him!" (Luke 11:13). Jesus was telling His disciples that the power of the Holy Spirit must be present in prayer. Without the Holy Spirit's presence and power, their prayers would be impotent. Jesus was saying, in effect, "Your Father will give you the Holy Spirit. Let the Holy Spirit help you."

Paul further explains why the power of the Holy Spirit is necessary in prayer:

> The Spirit helps us in our weakness. We do not know what we ought to pray for, but the Spirit himself intercedes for us with groans that words cannot express. And he who searches our hearts knows the mind of the Spirit, because the Spirit intercedes for the saints in accordance with God's will.
>
> Romans 8:26–27

The more we understand the power of the Holy Spirit, the more dependent on Him we become. The more dependent we become, the more we pray and enjoy praying. Prayer is no longer a struggle of the flesh, as when the disciples in Gethsemane tried to pray but fell asleep.

We now understand why Jesus said, "The spirit is willing, but the body is weak" (Matthew 26:41; Mark 14:38). We must understand the power of the Holy Spirit in prayer. As

168

we achieve victory over the flesh by the power of the Spirit, we can pray.

God's Will in Action

Let us ask you a question: Where can we see God's will in action?

Answer: On earth.

On earth is the context for our lives. When we say to God, "May Your will be done on earth," it reminds us that the only place God can transform our lives is right here where we live. When we say *on earth*, it means this gently tilting planet. It concerns the salvation, discipleship and transformation of human beings right here. Even more than this, it involves the healing and restoration of all mankind. Because of this, the Lord's Prayer contains those two important words *on earth*.

The will of God on earth is for the well-being of humanity. The Lord Jesus Christ, Creator of earth and all life, declared, "When you pray, pray for the will of God in the context of the earth." But where does this begin? It begins in my personal life. I cannot pray the words *Your will be done on earth* without being affected by them.

As a person who prays this prayer, I, Alemu, start right at the beginning of the Lord's Prayer with the words *my Father*. I stand on the Father-child relationship already established with God: "My Father, who is in heaven." I recognize His Fatherhood. I never say my prayer to anyone who happens to be out there. Rather, I call to my heavenly Father. I acknowledge that I belong to Him on earth. When I pray for God's will to be done on earth, I am asking God for His will to be done in my life: "Lord, I am willing to understand Your will, submit to it and fulfill it. Lord God, Your will is the most important thing in my life."

Your will be done on earth is a prayer that begins at the personal level. Whatever we pray, we cannot pray for others unless we have a personal relationship with God and the commitment, responsibility and determination to carry out God's will, beginning with ourselves. Otherwise, it is a prayer of the Pharisees; it means nothing. We are only repeating words. When I say *Your will be done on earth*, I am acknowledging that it starts with me, recognizing and accepting the will of God for my life.

My prayer for God's will on earth, then, moves naturally into my circles of affection. I ask God for His will to be done in my family, ministry, friendships, hopes and dreams; everything that relates to me. *Let Your will be done* is the most dangerous prayer that one can pray. We must not pray it lightly. When we ask, "God, may Your will be done in my personal life and everything I touch," the power of God is unleashed like a rushing river, dynamic and life altering. It is not something tentative or hesitant; it is mighty. Nothing can stop the will of God.

When you pray to live in the context of the Kingdom, you are saying, "Lord, I don't just want to live in a dynamic Kingdom; I want to be a dynamic person for Your glory. I want to be a life-altering person for Your Kingdom. I can't be simply lukewarm." When you pray *Your will be done on earth*, you are saying, "I want to be a Kingdom builder; a mighty person for Your purposes."

His Will for All the Earth

The Word says that "the earth will be filled with the glory of God." We are asking for this when we ask that His will be done on earth. If we stop and think about it, we are asking God to fulfill His promises from the prophecies revealed in Scripture. Jesus is the mighty prophet of God who spoke only truth—dynamic truth.

Jesus foretold that the Gospel of the Kingdom would be preached to every creature on earth. We are asking for this when we ask for His will to be done on earth. We are saying, "God, let what You said (Jesus' prophetic word) be fulfilled." We are giving an amen to the prophecy of Christ: "Let it be so, God. What You have written in Your Word, let it be done. Let it take place and be fulfilled in us on earth and through all humanity." We are asking for the glory of the Lord to be revealed, and all flesh to see it together.

The apostle Paul reminds us that creation itself groans, awaiting the fulfillment of the Kingdom. When we pray that His will be done on earth, we are standing with all creation, desiring that everything created for His glory will bring Him glory. Everything was created by Him and for Him. When we say *Your will be done on earth*, we are saying, "Show who You are—Your wisdom, power, might, care, love and compassion. Lord, let it be so. Let the world be enlightened!"

When we pray this, we are broadening our concerns beyond family issues, personal ministry issues or even Church issues. When we say *Your will be done on earth*, we are removing the fence from around us. We are telling God that we recognize and are committing to two things:

- His will
- The extent of His will—something that knows no bounds

171

Praying this dangerous prayer pushes us beyond ourselves, beyond our circumstances and experiences. We are asking God to stretch and expand our territory. If we are truly able to say *Your will be done on earth as it is in heaven*, we are no longer limited by ethnicity, social status, circumstances or things visible or invisible. We are saying we are willing to go beyond any limits. We are willing to cross over and leave our comfort zones. We still pray for our own personal concerns, but we also embrace in prayer the entire earth and everything God created.

This is the most powerful prayer in the Bible for reaching out to the world with the Gospel. This is why the Lord gave us this pattern. He is painting us a picture and expanding our vision. Jesus led the disciples step-by-step to

- Establish a relationship with the Father before praying
- Recognize where the Father is—He is in heaven above
- Understand that God is exalted
- Recognize, adore and worship God's name
- Ask for His Kingdom in heaven to come down

Once we have said this, we can no longer limit God to our own small areas of concern. We are asking Him to manifest His glory on earth. If we look at earth, what do we see? Sin. Death. Sickness. Darkness. A person who wants to see what is on earth needs only to listen to the news. In spite of all this, Jesus says: "Now ask for the will of God to take place on earth. Let it start in you and then spread to the rest of the world."

The Divine Pattern

Next, after asking God for His will to be done here on earth, Jesus said we ask God to accomplish His will on earth "as it is in heaven." We ask God for His will to be done according to the heavenly pattern. God's heavenly pattern is perfect because it is not sinful or distorted by earthly human views.

God always furnishes the pattern when He wants to start something new, divine, mighty and powerful. Look at the examples we have studied. When God wanted to save humanity during Noah's time, He told His servant to build an ark and provided detailed specifications. He wanted Noah to do on earth just what was patterned in heaven. Noah followed God's instructions, and the Ark became a refuge, a place where lives were saved. God's pattern for earth was the same as it was in heaven. It was complete.

We recall that when the Lord wanted the Israelites to know how to worship Him, he called Moses to the mountain and gave him a pattern for the Tabernacle; a heavenly pattern. God was clear with Moses: "Do according to what I have shown you. Don't change it. Don't try to understand all of it. Just do it according to what I've shown you on the mountain." The fact that Moses did according to what God commanded is repeated over and over in Scripture. When it was finished, the glory of the Lord filled the Tabernacle.

We recall as well that King David had a desire to build a Temple for the Lord, but the Lord said, "No, son, you've shed a lot of blood, and you aren't going to build Me a Temple." The Lord then promised David that his son would build the Temple. David advised young Solomon with this wisdom: "Son, I've received the pattern in detail from the Lord. This is how to build the Temple of the Lord so that God's desire will be done on earth. The glory of heaven will be manifested on earth in this Temple, so you must do it according to the pattern that God showed me." Solomon did, and the glory of the Lord came.

God has a divine pattern for every new or restored thing, and this includes prayer at our personal altars. For our prayers to be effective, they need to conform to the heavenly or divine pattern. The Lord Jesus said this in the gospel of John: "My Father tells Me what to say and how to say it." This means there is a pattern for what to do and how to do it—including prayer. We need to ask God not only to give us success in doing His will, but also to give us the very pattern of His will. How does God want it done? Jesus said repeatedly that He did not do anything He had not seen His Father do. He was pointing to the divine pattern. Jesus watched for the heavenly pattern and followed it. When you pray, your prayer should be not only for God's will to be done on earth, but that it will be done as it is in heaven.

Today, the most neglected aspects of our ministries involve patterns and methods. We never think to ask the Lord for the pattern. We typically ask God for a vision, for what He wants to do, but often we do not ask how to do it. Jesus, in praying that God's will be done on earth as in heaven, was saying that we should ask for and know God's heavenly pattern.

The Pattern for God's Children

In heaven everything is perfect. The model is perfect and it is followed perfectly. When we ask that "Your will be done on earth, as it is in heaven," we are asking the Lord for perfection, for the Lord to do His will—and not just for ministries or activities He has asked us to do. At its heart, it is a prayer that asks Him to lead and guide us into holiness. That is why the Bible says to be holy as our Father in heaven is holy.

When God looks at His children, there is a pattern He wants to see. How do we know? It is written in Romans 8.

The plan of God is for every child of God to be conformed and changed into the likeness of Jesus Christ. That is the heavenly pattern. The life of Jesus was not an earthly pattern; it was a heavenly pattern. The Word became flesh and dwelt among us; God showed us what the pattern looks like.

One of Jesus' disciples turned to Him one day and said, "Jesus, show us the Father and that's enough for us."

The Lord Jesus replied, "Haven't you seen the Father? You've been with Me a long time. Haven't you seen Him?"

He meant they had seen the pattern. *He* was the pattern, the perfect pattern of how to live in holiness. Jesus showed them the Father by His words, His life, the way He ministered and how He touched people. Jesus' life reflected and demonstrated the Father.

Paul also encourages us to live our lives after the pattern of Jesus:

> Since, then, you have been raised with Christ, set your hearts on things above, where Christ is seated at the right hand of God. Set your minds on things above, not on earthly things. For you died, and your life is now hidden with Christ in God. When Christ, who is your life, appears, then you also will appear with him in glory.
>
> Colossians 3:1–4

Paul tells believers to live life on earth according to the heavenly pattern, which is how God intends us to live it. That is how we become radical for God. We do not remain satisfied with the earthly standard, because we set our lives and ministry on what we have seen in the heavenlies. How do we know the pattern? We know through the Word of God, the life of Jesus Christ and the inspiration and revelation of the Holy Spirit.

Three Powerful Phrases

These three phrases we have been studying are interrelated and provide a full picture of what we are to ask God for at the altar of worship and prayer:

- Your Kingdom come
- Your will be done
- On earth as it is in heaven

By doing this we acknowledge His place in the heavenlies and recognize that His name is holy and exalted. At that point we are ready to understand His Kingdom purpose, discover His will and pray that it be fulfilled on earth according to His perfect heavenly pattern.

How? What pattern? Follow the heavenly pattern even in seeking a pattern: *Ask! Seek! Knock!* It will be opened to you.

QUESTIONS FOR REFLECTION

1. Why did the disciples ask Jesus to teach them how to pray? If you had been one of the disciples, would you have asked the same? Why?

2. How do you rekindle the fire in your life, family, workplace or organizations that are important to you?

3. Reflect on your plans and determine if all is for Kingdom purposes.

13

Decree Using Bold Prayers

In teaching His disciples to pray, Jesus gave clear guidance that it begins with relationship. As our hearts burn with passion to know our heavenly Father, it follows naturally that we experience the heartfelt desire to see His Kingdom come, His will be done, and His will be done on earth as it is in heaven.

That foundation of prayer, a relationship with the Living God, results in true worship at the altar. True worship leads into true understanding of God's purpose, which results in obedience. When we recognize that foundation and the power of prayer, it is natural to ask Him for what we need. Our God is the Lord who cares and supplies the needs of His children abundantly.

In giving His disciples the Lord's Prayer, Jesus was teaching us not only where to start but also what to ask for. Let us look at these principles briefly.

Give Us Today Our Daily Bread

Jesus puts our asking within very specific boundaries: *today.* We should learn to depend upon God for daily needs. When we know our needs and go to Him according to His Word, God is more than willing to provide them: "If you remain in me and my words remain in you, ask whatever you wish, and it will be given you" (John 15:7).

Man does not live by bread alone. The extent of this phrase is much larger and deeper than the literal food and clothing we need. When we ask for daily bread, we are also asking for divine provisions that enable us to fulfill God's purpose in our lives and help us experience the abundant life Jesus promised (see John 10:10). We need God's provision in our personal endeavors, our families, ministries, churches and communities; all are included in "give us today our daily bread." This prayer speaks to these two key areas:

1. Basic Necessities

Food, clothing and shelter are basic human needs. Jesus taught about this: "Your heavenly Father knows that you need them" (Matthew 6:32). When these basic needs are not met, we cannot live the fulfilled life Jesus promised. He created everything for our use. All the resources of the world are created for us; in turn, we are created for God's glory. Because of our relationship with the Father as His children, we are able to come to Him with boldness and ask Him to provide for our daily physical needs.

2. Spiritual Needs

Our spiritual needs are included in "daily bread." God gives us permission to ask Him to provide for all our spiritual needs, starting with our salvation. We come to Him every day for His forgiveness and mercy; mercies that are new each morning. His grace is available for the asking, bringing all the provision of God to bear in our lives: wisdom, knowledge, gifts and fruit of the Holy Spirit, spiritual renewal and victory. How wonderful to get up in the morning and say to almighty God, *My Father, please give me today . . .*

- The blessings I need to be a blessing to others
- Your grace to do Your will and bring glory to Your name
- Your anointing to fulfill Your purpose
- Your wisdom, understanding and knowledge to live wholeheartedly for You
- The gifts and power of Your Holy Spirit to advance Your Kingdom and to be a better leader, spouse, parent, child, friend, neighbor
- All the spiritual blessings You promised to live a life worthy of Your calling (see Ephesians 1:3)
- Revelation of Your holy Word

Give us today our daily bread includes all these and more. It is a blank check with the signature of our Lord and Savior that invites us to fill in our needs. Remember, God gives in proportion to the openness of our hearts and blesses us according to His purpose. When on the altars of our hearts we freely offer Him praise, adoration and worship, then we freely receive what we need for life and godliness:

"I know the plans I have for you," declares the LORD, "plans to prosper you and not to harm you, plans to give you hope and a future. Then you will call upon me and come and pray to me, and I will listen to you. You will seek me and find me when you seek me with all your heart. I will be found by you," declares the LORD.

Jeremiah 29:11–14

Forgive Our Debts

Asking for forgiveness of sin and cleansing is part of the daily Christian walk. This starts with confession of any known sin in our lives. God is a forgiving God, but we have to go to Him with heartfelt repentance. Since repentance means changing the direction of our hearts and minds, it enables us to stay in agreement and right relationship with God. That is why the Word of God encourages us to "be renewed in the spirit of your mind" (Ephesians 4:23 NKJV). Lasting change can take place only when we exercise a renewed mind, pure motives and a clean heart.

Remember: One of the things that destroys the altar of God and kills the fire is unconfessed sin, for it leads to disobedience and rebelliousness. The pendulum swing of forgiveness is vital for us to understand:

- *We must be willing to recognize sin and confess it in our lives.* The Word of God says simply, "If we confess our sins, he is faithful and just and will forgive us our sins and purify us from all unrighteousness" (1 John 1:9). Confessing sin requires humility of heart. God certainly does not despise a broken and repentant heart (see Psalm 51:17). Rather, He rejoices over it.

- *Then as we experience God's forgiveness for our sins, the pendulum swings back, and we are challenged to forgive others.* Forgiving others brings healing and freedom to our lives. That is the reason the Lord Jesus taught us to say, "Forgive us our debts, as we forgive our debtors." Forgiving others may not be an easy thing to do, but it is essential for keeping our altars pure and the fire burning.

> "Therefore, if you are offering your gift at the altar and there remember that your brother has something against you, leave your gift there in front of the altar. First go and be reconciled to your brother; then come and offer your gift."
>
> Matthew 5:23–24

Do Not Lead Us into Temptation

God's command and direction for His children is to be holy as He is holy. Receiving forgiveness from the Lord by confessing our sins is the first step.

Holiness means being set apart to God as well as for God. A person cannot walk in holiness in his or her own strength. As God the Father sent His Son to cover our sins and iniquities by His blood, He also sent His Holy Spirit to give us victory over sin every day. To overcome sin and live a holy life, the Spirit's leading is essential.

When Jesus told His disciples to pray in this manner, "Do not lead us into temptation," He was telling them to ask God not to leave them to their own desires. James makes this point clearly:

> When tempted, no one should say, "God is tempting me." For God cannot be tempted by evil, nor does he tempt anyone; but each one is tempted when, by his own evil desire, he is

dragged away and enticed. Then, after desire has conceived, it gives birth to sin; and sin, when it is full-grown, gives birth to death.

James 1:13–15

The core of this phrase is asking God to deliver us from ourselves. The most challenging thing we face is the decision to overcome our own desires or die to sin. When the enemy comes, we can command and resist him in the name of Jesus. He has no choice but to flee. When people try to trap us, we can run away from them. But we cannot rebuke or run away from our flesh. Our flesh is overcome only by the power of the Holy Spirit.

Temptation is all around us. We need deliverance from the love of money, which is the root of all evil. We need to be delivered from the temptations that stem from lust of the eyes and pride of life. We need God's strength against boasting and greed (see 1 John 2:16; Galatians 5:19–21).

We need the leading of the Holy Spirit of God every day: "If the Spirit leads you, then you are not subject to the Law" (Galatians 5:18 GNT).

The fastest way to quench the fire of the Holy Spirit is by yielding to the desires of the flesh. Asking God for deliverance from temptation is a sound strategy in your daily life to keep the altar intact and the fire burning.

Deliver Us from the Evil One

According to the *International Standard Bible Encyclopedia*, the Hebrew word for *deliver* means "to set free, save, cause to escape, draw out or recover." In Greek *deliver* means "to rescue, discharge or save." Our God is a deliverer! When we

pray to God for deliverance, we address the following four
areas:

1. *Deliverance from the Past*

Deliverance begins with our salvation; we are set
free from condemnation. God delivers us from the
consequences of sin, eternal death and hell. He sets
the captives free from the power of death and gives
us eternal life. God saves, rescues, draws out, grants
favor and brings forth by giving everyone who calls
upon His name spiritual resurrection and a place in
His family.

This includes deliverance not only from sin but
also from the guilt of past sin. The evil one is crafty
in his use of guilt to hold us back from enjoying freedom in our salvation and reaching our destinies. The
guilt of the past can be a tremendous obstacle to
the glory of the future. When God delivers us from
the guilt of past failures, we forget what lies behind
and press on to the glory of God.

2. *Deliverance from the Power of Sin*

The second aspect of God's deliverance is libera-
tion from the power of sin and the trap of the evil
one, Satan. One of the New Testament definitions
of *deliver*—"make useless or without effect"—refers
to this. By empowering His children, the Lord makes
the weapons of the evil one useless, without effect:
"In that coming day no weapon turned against you
will succeed" (Isaiah 54:17 NLT). Jesus Himself said,
"I have given you authority to trample on snakes
and scorpions and to overcome all the power of the
enemy; nothing will harm you" (Luke 10:19).

When praying for the Lord to deliver us from the evil one, we are declaring and accepting the position and authority God has given us as His children. The apostle John wrote these words to young Christians: "I write to you, young men, because you have overcome the evil one. . . . I write to you, young men, because you are strong, and the word of God lives in you, and you have overcome the evil one" (1 John 2:13–14).

3. *Deliverance from the Schemes of the Evil One*
Every day we need God's divine guidance and protection to discern and avoid the enemy's schemes. These come in many forms and shapes, through many different means and challenges. The evil one is the father of lies, deceit and deception. We stand in daily need of understanding, wisdom and discernment. God has already broken the enemy's trap, but we need to know that in order to walk in victory: "We have escaped like a bird from a hunter's trap; the trap is broken, and we are free!" (Psalm 124:7 GNT).

4. *The Ongoing Protection of God*
The enemy is defeated, but he always tries to strike or attack through intimidation, like a roaring lion. But the Lion of Judah, Jesus Christ who is in us and with us, is greater than the defeated enemy who tries to threaten us (see 1 John 4:1–6). Psalm 91:7 tells us that the evil ones fall on our left and right and cannot come near us: "A thousand may fall at your side, ten thousand at your right hand, but it will not come near you."

God, Our Deliverer

God is our deliverer, setting us free from the past, protecting us today and leading us from victory to victory. There are many, many promises in Scripture of His protection and deliverance. He is our Father, Good Shepherd, Guide, Light, Shield, Strong Tower and so much more. How does this daily protection take place? God protects His children through many means, including these:

- *His Name*

  The name of the Lord Jesus Christ is our best protection. Jesus Himself said this in His prayer for the disciples: "Holy Father, protect them by the power of your name—the name you gave me—so that they may be one as we are one. While I was with them, I protected them and kept them safe by that name you gave me" (John 17:11–12). The name of the Lord is our strongest tower of protection (see Proverbs 18:10).

- *The Power of the Blood*

  The blood of the Lord Jesus Christ is the source of our deliverance and our protection. Remember that on the eve of their deliverance from Egypt, God told the Israelites to put blood on the top and sides of the doorframes of their homes in order to be protected. He said, "The blood will be a sign for you on the houses where you are; and when I see the blood, I will pass over you. No destructive plague will touch you when I strike Egypt" (Exodus 12:13). Moses said, "When the LORD goes through the land to strike down the Egyptians, he will see the blood . . . and will pass over that doorway, and he will not permit the destroyer to enter your houses and strike you down" (Exodus 12:23).

In the New Testament we are saved, washed and set free by the blood of the Lamb. There is truly wonderworking power in the blood of the Lord Jesus Christ: "They overcame [Satan] by the blood of the Lamb" (Revelation 12:11).

• *The Holy Spirit*

God protects us by the power of the Holy Spirit who lives in us. God is in us and for us. The enemy cannot touch us. According to Scripture we are temples of the Holy Spirit. He protects us, therefore, through His seal of ownership on our lives.

• *His Presence*

God protects us by His presence. He is Immanuel, God with us. Jesus said He will not leave or forsake us. We are under the shadow of His wings (see Psalm 91). That was the reason David could say with confidence, "Even though I walk through the valley of the shadow of death, I will fear no evil, for you are with me; your rod and your staff, they comfort me" (Psalm 23:4).

• *His Word*

Jesus defeated the evil one during the wilderness temptation by the Word (see Matthew 4:1–11; Ephesians 6:10–18). God protects us by the power of His Word. When we speak of "the Word of God," we are referring to every promise and covenant God has given us. The writer of Hebrews tells us that the Word of God is "sharper than any double-edged sword" (Hebrews 4:12). With it, we fight and over-come the enemy.

In order to keep the fire of the altar alive and strong, we ask God not only for His provision and leading but also for deliverance. Without the deliverance of God, the enemy will try to destroy our altars just as he did the physical stones and bronze structures of Old Testament times. Only through the protection of God are we able to live a life of freedom and avoid the schemes of the evil one.

When we understand the victory we have in Christ, we can come boldly before our heavenly Father with a heart of gratitude and worship and say, "Yours is the kingdom and the power and the glory forever. Amen" (Matthew 6:13 NKJV).

QUESTIONS FOR REFLECTION

1. The Lord's Prayer teaches us to pray with His divine pattern. Have you established a passionate divine pattern?

2. Explain how important forgiveness is to your relationship with your heavenly Father.

3. In your own Christian life, how important is deliverance? How does deliverance help a believer experience the ever-increasing fire of prayer and worship?

14

Keep the Fire Burning

I, Chuck, remember telling a friend of mine once, "If the fire of God and His Spirit left me, I would crumble to the ground!"

The friend promptly replied, "If that happened to me, I am not sure I would even recognize a change in my life."

This is not what the Lord wants to be the norm in our lives. He wants the fire to fall and burn brightly so we can experience the fullness of His provision, protection and guidance. He wants us to make a lasting impact for the Kingdom.

The Consuming Fire

Scripture describes our God as fire: "For the LORD your God is a consuming fire, a jealous God" (Deuteronomy 4:24; see Hebrews 12:29).

Fire is the indicator or the display of the glory and the majesty of almighty God, the One we are invited to worship.

He dwells in unapproachable glorious light. Furthermore, the fire of God is a sign of His righteous judgment against his foes: "Fire goes before him and consumes his foes on every side" (Psalm 97:3).

The fire of God, therefore, creates in us holy fear so that we can come into His presence with reverence and know that He goes before us with His righteous judgment to protect us and give us victory as we worship Him.

God shows this aspect of His nature in His dealings with man in both Old Testament and New.

Moses' ministry of setting the people free from slavery and bringing them to the Promised Land of covenant started with the fire of God's presence on the mountain of Horeb in a bush: "There the angel of the LORD appeared to him in flames of fire from within a bush. Moses saw that though the bush was on fire it did not burn up. So Moses thought, 'I will go over and see this strange sight—why the bush does not burn up'" (Exodus 3:2–3).

Once Moses had brought the people out of slavery, God led them by fire:

> By day the LORD went ahead of them in a pillar of cloud to guide them on their way and by night in a pillar of fire to give them light, so that they could travel by day or night. Neither the pillar of cloud by day nor the pillar of fire by night left its place in front of the people.
>
> Exodus 13:21–22

God confirmed His presence with them by showing His glory on Mount Sinai: "To the Israelites the glory of the LORD looked like a consuming fire on top of the mountain" (Exodus 24:17). The Lord did not just send fire; He was there: "Mount Sinai was covered with smoke, because the Lord descended on it in fire" (Exodus 19:18).

God's burning presence was the reason that "in the fortieth year" of Israel's wanderings, as they were finally "about to cross the Jordan" into the Promised Land, Moses could tell the people of God confidently to "be assured today that the LORD your God is the one who goes across ahead of you like a devouring fire" (Deuteronomy 1:3; 9:1, 3).

Like Moses, John the Baptist pointed to the redemption of God's people by fire. John baptized with water those who repented and wanted to enter the coming Kingdom. Water baptism signifies the death of the old life in the flesh and separation to a new spiritual life in Christ Jesus; it is an act that symbolizes new life.

But John also knew that he was a forerunner for the coming Messiah: "I baptize you with water for repentance. But after me will come one who is more powerful than I, whose sandals I am not fit to carry. He will baptize you with the Holy Spirit and with fire" (Matthew 3:11).

The Messiah came, and having prepared His disciples, He gave them this order: "I am going to send you what my Father has promised; but stay in the city until you have been clothed with power from on high" (Luke 24:49).

The obedient disciples remained in Jerusalem. They waited in worship and prayer. Then on the Day of Pentecost, the fire of the Holy Spirit fell and launched the Church: "They saw what seemed to be tongues of fire that separated and came to rest on each of them" (Acts 2:3).

After that, the disciples began to declare the glory of God, resulting in the salvation of three thousand that day.

God's fire cleanses, sanctifies, beautifies and changes us into the likeness of His Son and prepares us for Kingdom work. After purifying us with His fire, God uses us as instruments of His glory, awakening our spirits, renewing our lives, breaking the chains of sin and burning down our selfish egos.

Everlasting life is a gift given to those who repent and believe in Jesus Christ. The fire of God follows salvation, empowering us for Kingdom life. Let us stand strong, welcoming the fire of God to purify our hearts.

The Result of God's Fire

Here to encourage you are eight of the many remarkable results of preparing your altar and welcoming the fire of God to fall:

1. The Fire Restores Holiness

One of the results in our lives of the fire of God is holiness. It cleanses the tongue, making His servants deserving speakers of the Lord. It cleanses our image, so we can reflect the life of the Lord.

Here is an example that illustrates this—the mining of gold and purifying it for the market. After digging in the ground and removing raw gold ore, which is mixed with many other elements, the miners put it into a container able to sustain very high temperatures. The fire that burns it is so intense that the dirt and other particles melt out of the gold ore. The melted gold then must cool to solidify. When it is cool, it is inspected. One of the initial ways the inspector determines whether it is pure gold is by its ability to reflect his face in the same way a mirror does. If it does not, he orders it to be fired again under high temperature. Once the gold has been proven pure, it goes to market for sale.

God's fire does the same thing in the lives of His children. It purifies and separates us from the dirt of the world. God's fire makes us clean, so we reflect His image (see 2 Corinthians 3:18). The fire of God fills our hearts with His presence and glory and makes us His temple (see 2 Chronicles 7:1–3): "For those God foreknew he also predestined to be conformed to the likeness of his Son, that he might be the firstborn among many brothers" (Romans 8:29).

2. The Fire Renews Our Spiritual Lives

Passion for prayer and worship and the desire to know and obey the Word of God are the result of true fire. When we lose the fire, we lose the essence of prayer and relationship with God. If we do not have fire, all we have is smoke, which has no power to make a difference. To illustrate this truth let me, Alemu, share a personal story about why I am a student of the Word of God.

The night I received my Bible and started reading it, I loved it so much I didn't want to stop reading. Before that, the first time a teacher asked me to share for school devotions, I didn't have a Bible. I had to borrow one and didn't know how to find a passage of Scripture. I didn't even know the difference between the Old and New Testaments. That day I made a decision to know the Scriptures. I also promised the Lord to keep my passion for the Word of God as long as I live.

I started ministry with a very high level of commitment and fire for the Word of God. After many years had passed, I was invited to speak at a conference in Rome. As I was flying to Rome, I started reading a book about the Word of God and worship. This was part of my research for a book I had just started writing in Amharic, an Ethiopian language, called *True Worship*.

I was settled in and enjoying the book, when I heard an inner voice say, *Stop reading.*

I was puzzled and stopped reading for a few minutes and started again. I heard the same voice. I started paying attention.

After a few minutes, the voice said, *Where are you going?*

I thought I had a wonderful answer, so I responded, "I am going to Rome."

The voice came back with another question, *Why do you go to Rome?*

"To speak at a spiritual conference."

There was silence for a few minutes. At this time, I knew the Lord was speaking to me. I started weeping, forgetting that I was surrounded by other passengers in a plane. The presence of the Lord was so real! I didn't know how to respond or how to be.

The voice then asked me, *Why do you preach My Word? Do you preach it because you know how to preach, or do you preach because you love My Word?*

I lost it! I was reminded about the night I received my Bible, and the first time I preached by borrowing a Bible.

When I arrived in Rome, the pastor who had invited me arrived to pick me up and asked if I would like to stop to eat.

I replied, "No, but thank you. Just take me to the hotel."

After he dropped me off, he asked me what time I would like to be picked up for dinner. I told him that I would not need dinner and to come back tomorrow.

As soon as he left, I was on my face on the floor. I didn't change my clothes. As I was repenting and praying, I fell asleep. At two a.m., I was awakened and told by a voice to read Leviticus 6:8–13.

I opened my Bible to the passage and read it. Three times the same warning and command was given to the Levites. *Do not let the fire go out on the altar of God.*

That night I understood the importance of keeping the fire burning.

One of the greatest challenges during the journey toward prophetic destiny is keeping the fire burning. When the fire of love, the Holy Spirit, holiness, worship, the Word of God and ministry have burned out, the journey is simply a desire without lasting impact, a strong wish without true break-through. A person can have a "title" in the Kingdom, but without the fire it is not possible to fulfill everything that goes along with the title.*

3. The Fire Leads to Repentance

Whenever the people of God witnessed the fire of God falling on the altar, they knelt—or dropped to the ground—in worship. This was the case, for instance, with the fire falling on the altar at the Tabernacle and at the Temple. We learned in our study of Elijah's monumental rebuilding of an altar that the people saw and believed the Lord is the God who answers by fire. Those who doubted were satisfied and realized that God possesses the might attributed to Him. That appearance of fire from heaven brought idolaters to their knees and put everything under the glory of God: "When all the people saw this, they fell prostrate and cried, 'The LORD—he is God! The LORD—he is God!'" (1 Kings 18:39).

---

*This material is taken from Alemu Beeftu, Ph.D., *Breakout for Breakthrough: Journey for Prophetic Destiny* (Alemu Beeftu, 2019), 37–39, and is used by permission.

4. The Fire Consumes the Sacrifice

Let's continue with images from Elijah's altar, since they give us such a good visual understanding of the result of God's fire: "The fire of the LORD fell and burned up the sacrifice, the wood, the stones and the soil, and also licked up the water in the trench" (1 Kings 18:38). We learn that the first thing the fire of God does is to consume our lives. This is because our lives are the sacrifices offered to Him. The apostle Paul urges us to present our bodies to the Lord as living sacrifices (see Romans 12:1). The fire of God begins not with our service, but with our lives. If we really want God to use us, then we must first give ourselves to Him.

5. The Fire Consumes the Wood

Having consumed the sacrifice, the fire also consumes the wood. This wood may symbolize our gifting, but it also symbolizes our fears, doubts and weaknesses. The fire of God sanctifies not only our lives but also the gifts of grace we have received from Him. All of our gifts, as well as our lives, belong to Him. This allows us to be used in service to His glory.

6. The Fire Consumes the Stones

Stone is not easily consumed by fire. But God's fire burns that which cannot be burned and melts that which cannot be melted. The stones are the very foundation of sacrifice. These stones may symbolize our knowledge, experience, call, ministry and all that we claim to be unshakable and permanent. It includes what we have and what we desire to have. When the fire of God comes, everything will be consumed by it.

After being touched by the fire of His glory, we will say, "I saw God face-to-face, and my body is healed." After Jacob wrestled with God and sought His blessing in a life-changing encounter, he "called the place Peniel, saying, 'It is because I saw God face to face, and yet my life was spared. The sun rose above him as he passed Peniel'" (Genesis 32:30–31).

The fire melts our stony hearts and changes us, so we resemble Christ Jesus. It enables us to see not only our limits, but also God's beauty and mercy. Having understood this fact, Paul wrote that he considered everything loss compared to the surpassing greatness of knowing Jesus Christ,

that I may gain Christ and be found in him, not having a righteousness of my own that comes from the law, but that which is through faith in Christ—the righteousness that comes from God and is by faith. I want to know Christ and the power of his resurrection and the fellowship of sharing in his sufferings, becoming like him in his death, and so, somehow, to attain to the resurrection from the dead.

Philippians 3:8–11

If all this is true, it is necessary for us to invite God's fire to consume us, along with our sacrifices and wood and stones. We cannot see His might and glory otherwise. Boasting to have gifts and experience without the fire of God is the same as collecting lamps but sitting in darkness.

7. *The Fire Consumes the Soil*

The soil or the earth supported the stones of the altar and the sacrifice. The fire of God consumed the soil along with the meat, wood and stones. The soil may symbolize things that we consider stable, firm, unchangeable or enduring. It may represent family, close relatives and friends, companions, a tribe, language, country and all those things we expect always to be the same.

Since the fire of God knows no boundaries, it consumes not only our lives and gifts, but also the soil on which we stand. When the fire of God consumes the earth, the land is cleansed of all concealed and invisible contaminants. Idols are burned up.

Moses and Joshua were told that the soil on which they stood was sanctified. This means that the person of God who wants to see the glory of God and inherit the Promised Land also must allow his tribe, land, culture, language and country to be touched by God's fire.

8. The Fire Consumes the Water

Water extinguishes fire. When we see a fire that is out of control, we instinctively run to get water. We could say that water is an enemy of fire. But when the fire of God comes, it consumes even water.

This means that when the fire of the Holy Spirit ignites us, we must submit everything to that fire because it annihilates everything that is an obstacle to God's work and glory. In other words, God's fire not only prepares us for His work, it also consumes whatever stands in His way. That is why it is frequently written in the Bible that the battle belongs to God. It is only He who can destroy fire with fire. If we submit to Him in everything and live for His glory, He is the One who fights for us and stays by our side in all circumstances. His fire breaks the chains of bondage and consumes our enemies (see Daniel 3). God's fire even melts the mountain that stands in our way (see Zechariah 4).

The fact that God's fire consumes water also shows us that when the glory of God is revealed, those things impossible by human effort and ability become very simple accomplishments for God. He is not governed by nature; on the contrary, God governs nature. He is not limited or bound by anything.

When the fire of God descends, there is only one thing we can do. Like the people of Israel who witnessed God's power as the fire fell, we cry, "The Lord—He is God! The Lord—He is God!"

We hope that the teaching in this book has activated within you that hunger to pray for, embrace and keep the fire of God. Be assured that it will annihilate every obstacle in the way of the dynamic Gospel. It will prove the vanity of idols.

As you witness the fire and its sanctifying power, we believe you will want to bow and declare your gratitude to our great God. God is your Savior. He is your Healer. He is your Redeemer. He is your Light. He is your Life. He is your Hope. He is your Shield. He is your Security. May you worship His majesty as you rekindle the altar fire and keep it burning.

Let us close with a song we wrote here at Glory of Zion International:

Let It Burn

There's a fire burning in the dead of night
It's a comin' for you with a voice of thunder
Shadows run from its dancing light
Stronger than the river that's pulling you under
It'll burn your flesh 'til your bones ignite
Strip you bare 'til you're on your knees
Leaves you hungry, makes you feel alive
Open your heart; can you feel it?

Let it burn, burn, burn; Light the way with the
furnace of desire
Let it burn, burn, burn; Don't resist the flame of His
fire

The Lord's comin' down in a roaring blaze
Sparks are gonna catch, light the world on fire
He's lookin' for the place where the devil plays
He's mad as hell, can you hear His choir?
He'll burn until no darkness remains
Angels marchin' right by His side
The saved are gonna rise, gonna sing His praise
Get on your feet and be counted

Holy fire, consume my soul; Light my feet, let my
spirit glow
Drown me in the flames so deep; Fill my lungs 'til
You're all I breathe

Let it burn

Light a match, spread the word, spill the oil, share
what you've heard
Tell the world He's comin' in flames and He won't
relent until you know His name*

*"Let it Burn" on *A Time to Advance—The Music of the Months* (Corinth, Tex.: Glory of Zion International Ministries, Inc., 2013). Words by Tracey Liggett and Justin Rana, music by Justin Rana. Used by permission.

QUESTIONS FOR REFLECTION

1. Review the eight results of the fire of God falling on the altar. Which of those results would you most like to have applied to your life?

2. What increases your desire to rekindle the altar fire? What hinders your desire? How can you remove the obstacles that keep you from a deepening desire to pray and worship?

3. How do God's provision, forgiveness, strength and deliverance help keep the altar fire burning?

Charles D. "Chuck" Pierce serves as president of Global Spheres, Inc. (GSI) in Corinth, Texas. Located in the Global Spheres Center, this apostolic, prophetic ministry is being used to gather and mobilize the worshiping Triumphant Reserve throughout the world. GSI facilitates other ministries as well and participates in regional and national gatherings to develop new Kingdom paradigms. Chuck also serves as president of Glory of Zion International Ministries, a ministry that aligns Jew and Gentile. He is known for his accurate prophetic gifting, which helps direct nations, cities, churches and individuals in understanding the times and seasons in which we live. Chuck and his wife, Pam, have six children and fifteen grandchildren.

FB: chuckdpierce
Twitter: @chuckdpierce
Instagram: @chuckdpierce

Dr. Alemu Beeftu, founder and president of Gospel of Glory, has a heart for training pastors, businessmen and politicians, with a goal of building national leadership infrastructures. Alemu presently works with transformational leaders of various ages in 54 countries who have the calling, gifting and character to foster sustainable societal change for the Kingdom of God.

A native of Ethiopia, Alemu earned a B.A. from Biola University and master's and doctoral degrees in curriculum design and community development from Michigan State University. More than thirty years of practice in these and related fields have made him an accomplished and sought-after leadership trainer. He also continues to provide leadership worldwide for the Body of Christ.

Alemu's most recently authored books include *Optimize Your Potential*; *Go Back to Go Forward*; *Breakout for Breakthrough*; *Divine Pattern for the Fullness of His Glory*; *God's Questions*; *Restoration for Lasting Transformation*; *Igniting Leaders for Kingdom Impact*; *Wrestling for Your Prophetic Destiny*; *Put Your Heart above Your Head*; *Leadership Journey*; *Spiritual Accountability and Leading for Kingdom Impact*; and *Determination to Make a Difference*. Learn more at www.goglory.org.

More from
Chuck D. Pierce

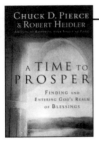

Prosperity is unleashed when you enter into the fullness of God's plan for your life. When you submit to His plan, He opens doors of abundance. In these pages, you will discover the biblical model for work, worship and giving, and understand how this pattern prepares you to give and receive blessings.

A Time to Prosper with Robert Heidler

This step-by-step handbook presents three bestselling spiritual warfare books in one practical volume. *When God Speaks* will help you discern God's guidance. *Prayers That Outwit the Enemy* exposes Satan's strategies. *Protecting Your Home from Spiritual Darkness* gives ten steps to keep evil locked out. Let this proven battle plan lead you to victory!

The Spiritual Warfare Handbook with Rebecca Wagner Sytsema